EXTREME ADVENTURES

ADVENTURES

Hawaii

BRAD OLSEN

HUNTER

HUNTER PUBLISHING, INC.
130 Campus Drive, Edison NJ 08818-7816, USA
Tel (732) 225 1900; Fax (732) 417 1744
E-mail: hunterpub@emi.net

1220 Nicholson Road, Newmarket, Ontario L3Y 7V1, CANADA
Tel (800) 399 6858; Fax (800) 363 2665

ISBN 1-55650-809-3
© 1998 Hunter Publishing

ViSiT OUR WEBSiTE!

For complete information about the hundreds of other travel guides available from Hunter Publishing, visit us online at:

www.hunterpublishing.com

This guide focuses on recreational activities. As all such activities contain elements of risk, the publisher, author, affiliated individuals and companies disclaim any responsibility for any injury, harm, or illness that may occur to anyone through, or by use of, the information in this book. Every effort has been made to ensure the accuracy of information in this book, but the publisher and author do not assume, and hereby disclaim, liability to any party for any loss or damage caused by errors, omissions, misleading information or any potential problem caused by information in this guide, even if these are a result of negligence, accident or any other cause.

Cover Photo: Leo de Wys
Images on page 85 and 92 by Tom Peloquin; image on page 51 by Ekaterina Nagornaia; all other photos and artwork by author.

Dedication

This book is dedicated to every person who has his or her own life in absolute control. Extreme adventures require skill, confidence, and the ability to understand one's own limits. Whereas physical fitness and a proper diet prepare the body for adventure, education and conservation are the keys to our collective survival. Be a part of the dynamic energy flow in your life and give thanks to the amazing wonders this planet affords us!

Acknowledgments

Many thanks to all who aided me in my pursuit to get this book out. Publisher Michael Hunter for putting up with my rookie moves; my parents (Elaine, Marshall, Susan) and relatives (brother Chris, sister Marsi, the Hausmans, Grandma O) for their continued encouragement; Nikki Kirkhart and Mark Maxam for their initial support; fellow travel writers Mike McColl, Bruce Northam and Robert Young Pelton for speaking-tour direction; Tom Peloquin and Tom Nardini and the whole C.O.R.E. Hawaii troop; my techno-family and friends at the CCC Warehouse (Consortium of Collective Consciousness); and to all my buddies in Chicago, San Francisco, and Planet Earth who fill me with the best gift of all – laughter. But most of all, thanks go to you, the reader. Thank you for buying this book and understanding the way to fun alternative travel excursions.

When the best student hears about the way
He practices it assiduously;
When the average student hears about the way
It seems to him one moment there and gone the next;
When the worst student hears about the way
He laughs out loud.
If he did not laugh it would not be worthy
of being the way.
Lao Tzu

About the Author

Brad Olsen grew up in the suburbs of Chicago, and graduated from Illinois State University in 1988 with a Marketing and Art degree. Rather than pursue a career in advertising, Brad treated himself to a summer of fun in Europe immediately following his collegiate commitments. This trip changed his life. Rather than chase the almighty dollar, Brad made a new commitment to chase the almighty fun. This meant there would be no career, no family, basically no commitments until he was well into his 30's.

Thus began one of the wildest and wackiest travel odysseys any young person could ever experience. After three fun-filled months on the European circuit, Brad returned to his hometown of Arlington Heights, Illinois and knew he had to move on. He packed up what he could, including his skis, and moved to Lake Tahoe, California just prior to the first snowfall. Without a place to stay or a job, Brad quickly made some core friends and landed a job selling skis for Heavenly Ski Resort within a week. After two winters and an extremely adventurous summer in Tahoe, Brad moved to the surf-town of Santa Cruz, California, where he spent six months drawing cartoons. He then headed out to Maui, Hawaii, selling activities for seven months. Nice life, huh? Well for Brad, the best was yet to come.

After leaving the Hawaiian Islands to attend his brother's wedding, Brad made a stopover at his adventure alma mater Lake Tahoe for some extreme skiing. A lady there told Brad of the teaching opportunities that awaited people like him in Japan. With no plans except to seek maximum fun in his 20's, Brad heeded this advice and bought a one-way ticket to Tokyo. It didn't take long before he found a job teaching conversational English in the beautiful and historic Japanese city of Kyoto. This provided our author the necessary funds to execute the ultimate adventure – a three-year trip around the world. Brad lived and worked in Japan for 14 months, then started his overland journey across China. He was one of the first American travelers allowed into Vietnam, then he went onwards to Thailand, Malaysia, Indonesia, and Australia. Utilizing his cartooning skills, Brad drew portraits of tourists in Cairns, then hitchhiked down and around the whole continent. Moving on from Australia, Brad visited India for half a year, including a month in Nepal trekking in the mighty Himalayas. Finishing up his world tour, Brad climbed to the top of the Great Pyramid in Egypt, went on to Israel, then did another stint in Europe before returning once again to Chicago. The complete story of his world tour is a popular and award-winning website. Internet users set a bookmark at: http://www.stompers.com.

Two strong urges overcame Brad upon returning from his world tour. One was to return to California, and the other was to write a book describing everything it takes for a person to make a world tour of his or her own become a reality. The title is *World Stompers: A Guide to Travel Manifesto*, now in its third edition. Today Brad Olsen lives in a techno-warehouse in San Francisco with several travel buddies he met in India. Their fluorescent and holographic "Aware House" is called the Consortium of Collective Consciousness, and the group enjoys throwing and attending rave parties.

"No alien land in all the world has any deep, strong charm for me, but that one; no other land could so longingly and beseechingly haunt my sleeping and waking, through half a lifetime, as that one has done. Other things leave me, but it abides." – Mark Twain reflecting on his 1889 visit to Hawaii.

Disclaimer

The publisher and author of *Extreme Adventure Guides* do not promote or endorse the listed activities nor the places described to undertake such activities. The participation in what is herein described as "Extreme Adventures" carries with it the inherent risk of injury, or even death. As with all strenuous activities, it is recommended that you consult with your doctor before participating in any kind of radical excursion or sport. In addition, the publisher and author wish to make it known that some of the sports described in this book require the use of a license, and/or considerable expertise in such an activity. Thus, the reader should become familiar with the sport and the conditions of the place where the activity is to be performed in order to diminish the risks of undertaking such activities.

Finally, none of the outfitters, retail shops, publications, organizations, or instructional schools have paid any money to be included in this guide. They are listed as resources only.

Important Note to Scuba Divers

Do not dive for a 24-hour period before any flight. This includes helicopter tours and inter-island flights. The body needs at least a day to de-compress and discharge harmful nitrous oxide. Flying during this time period can activate decompression sickness, commonly known as "the bends."

Foreword

by Bruce Northam

My Hawaii debut was the first stopover on a 1987 circle-the-Pacific, 15-country tour. I had presumed that "the trip" would *begin* with the next leg, Japan, but I was wrong – luscious Hawaii seduced me. Many Americans don't comprehend that we hold tropical jewels beyond Key West, and never make it to the healthiest state. Breathe.

As far as travel writers go, Brad Olsen is the real thing; a wondrous collision of motivation, prudence and vagabond wildness. With a fan continuum extending from film director Oliver Stone to ethereal Hindi phantoms, Brad keeps the beat. The wander wisdom exemplified by a favorite passage from his first book, *World Stompers,* swirls right into the book now in your grasp.

"Life can be as carefree and boundless as you want it. You just have to want it."

As a fellow journalist, I'm jealous of the unwavering stream of globetrotting intelligence that is available to Brad at San Francisco's Consortium of Collective Consciousness (CCC) – his 4,000-sq.-foot home and communal art pad. His dual role at CCC as travel meccaman/landlord more than qualifies him to write guidebooks. My NYC support network doesn't extend much beyond modems and the waitress in the diner beneath my apartment.

Conduct the esoteric excursions that inhabit *Extreme Adventures Hawaii* on your journeys. Appreciate the locals and their island culture. And no matter what *they* say, Waikiki ain't *that* bad. Oh yeah, tip your cap to the sweet vibes in the Waipio Valley.

Bruce Northam is the Editor in Chief of *Student Travels Magazine*. As a travel writer, he is best known as the author of *The Frugal Globetrotter*. Northam has freelanced for a variety of publications including: *Details, Swing, Men's Journal,* and *Diesel*. Northam has also made numerous appearances on CNN's travel segments and lectures around the country on the topic of budget travel. When not on the road, Northam makes his home in New York City.

Contents

Contents

Contents

Contents

Contents

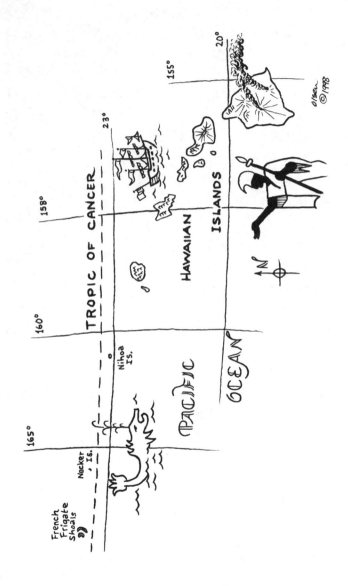

Introduction

Extreme Adventures. Author Brad Olsen knows them well. This series of high adrenaline guides is based on a Hawaiian adventure club the author participated in called C.O.R.E., which is an acronym for the Comrades Of Radical Excursions. The club has existed as an adventure group in Hawaii and California since 1986. C.O.R.E. was founded by a group of fun-loving 'comrades' with the sole purpose of bringing friends together for great outdoor adventures.

C.O.R.E. members at Seven Pools, Maui

Over 10 years later, C.O.R.E. is ready to expand its membership with a new series of guidebooks by Hunter called *Extreme Adventures*. Each guide will detail several dozen 'radical' excursions in a geographic area, complete with an adrenaline and risk meter for every one. Some of the adventures featured in this book are operated by outfitters, some are open to all in national and state parks, and some are known only to locals. Since most of the adventures included in this volume require a certain degree of physical fitness, it is necessary for the reader to first understand the disclaimer, then train to get into top physical shape. This book is not written for wimps or couch potatoes.

LAME EXCUSES

Let's get the lame excuses out of the way first. As mentioned in the *Introduction*, this book is not for lazy or non-physical people. You need a certain mind-set to get the most out of this book. That mentality is the "Go For It Attitude" or, like Paula Jones' jean promotion, "No Excuses." You have to be content to walk in the rain if that is the situation, get up early to catch the sunrise on Haleakala, work to master any given sport, and sometimes endure excruciating physical tests. All prima donnas please stay at the poolside.

Another barrier may be your own dear friends. Not everyone can do the things described in this book, and some will offer a litany of lame excuses rather than their full-spirited participation. Keep an ear out for the following and don't fall for any of them:

 ### I'M AFRAID OF SHARKS.
You should be if you are playing where they feed. Extreme adventurers should be aware that sharks

can smell blood from many miles away. The most dangerous shark situation occurs when they are tracking blood, which can lead to a feeding frenzy. The Hawaiian islands are rich in sea life and attract many varieties of sharks, including hammerheads. Fortunately, the type most often encountered by humans, the white-tip reef shark, is not dangerous unless seriously provoked. Let them be and they will let you be. Black wetsuited surfers have on rare occasions been mistaken for seals and munched upon, but the reality is that very few shark attacks have occurred anywhere in Hawaii (and only one or two have been fatal). So the odds are better that you will be struck by lightning than be bitten by a shark. Just avoid bleeding in the water and you shouldn't have to worry about an attack.

 I DON'T HAVE EQUIPMENT.

This depends entirely on the sports or activities you are into. You don't need much more than a pair of hiking boots to do a considerable number of the extreme adventures outlined in this book. By doing your radical excursions with outfitters, you are paying to go along with them and rent their equipment. Some sports require personal equipment, and if you think you will be doing the sport for years to come, it may be a good idea to make the investment.

⊚ I'M NOT IN GOOD SHAPE.

This is the lamest excuse. If you can't ride a
mountain bike or paddle a sea kayak, you have no
business reading this book. Put it down now. No
one can expect to be an expert at all of these
sports, let alone do them all. The idea is to strive,
no matter how many beers you had last night, to
give it your best. No bitching! Nobody likes a
winer, and if you are huffing and puffing on an
outback trail, maybe your body is trying to tell
you something. Pay attention, and start a work-
out program immediately.

⊚ IT COSTS TOO MUCH.

Some of the best things in life are free. This is
also the case with extreme adventures. Is there
an admission fee to ride a wave? A credit card
charge to trek in a pristine valley? A price tag on
a killer mountain bike ride? While some state and
national parks require a nominal admission and
camping fee, the real cost will be food and transportation – same as in the rat race. The activities
in this book that require an outfitter actually can
save you money, because then you don't have to
purchase the equipment yourself.

⊚ I DON'T KNOW ANYONE
WILLING TO JOIN ME.

This is a feeble excuse. Several of these sports
can be solo workouts, or can be started solo with

the good chance that new friends will be met along the way. If going with an outfitter, you will be part of an instant group. People doing extreme adventures are a gregarious and joyful lot. And why not? They are enjoying life at its fullest, and are very receptive to meeting other people of a like mind.

◎ I DON'T HAVE A VEHICLE.

Perfect! One less car in smoggy Hawaii is a damn good thing. Your karma points are going way up. Rather than think of what you can't do without a car, think of all the things you can do with a bike. Get a surfboard rack, or a bike cart for your wind-surf gear. Nobody has any excuses with a good mountain bike – they can even go where some 4WDs cannot. Remember, with the exception of the Big Island, the islands are not that big. Bicycles are a perfectly reasonable mode of transportation. Just look at China, which has as many bikes as people. Most airlines allow passengers to bring bikes as luggage for little or no extra cost.

ENVIRONMENTAL IMPACT

Okay, now that you have no excuses, it's time to start thinking of which radical excursion is right for you. But before you head out to the adventure paradise known as Hawaii, it is important you should consider your responsibility to the environment for all this fun you'll be having. It is pretty obvious when you look around that modern humans have had a profound effect on the natural ecosystems in this state. Some species, like the sandalwood and silversword, have been nearly wiped out. Other species are holding their own, but all deserve your utmost respect when you are encroaching upon their turf. Here are a few things to keep in mind to lessen or eliminate your own environmental impact:

Personal karma

Surfers and outdoor adventurers have to be some of the most ecologically minded people in the world. They notice, and put themselves at risk, every time their playground is tainted with another toxic accident. These sentient people have a great affinity for the planet because they are an integral part of it. We all are, but extreme adventurers put themselves on the line. There is nothing worse than an oil slick or a clear-cut forest to spoil the playful mood of the day.

Stomping trails

There are many rare plants in Hawaii that can be destroyed by your stepping on them. Hiking here can still be an extreme adventure – even on the trails.

Pack it in, pack it out

There is nothing as lame as coming upon a campsite and seeing it littered with someone else's junk. Remember, karma is a two-way street.

⊚ LET IT BE

Wasn't it cool when you discovered the cave stalactites? How about leaving everything exactly the way it was before you got there for the next adventurers to discover? Take only pictures, leave only footprints.

⊚ EDUCATE YOURSELF

One of the best ways to become an ecologically sound traveler is to educate yourself about the environment. Consider joining a club. Check the listings at the end of this book for a group that is right for you. Many of them sponsor inexpensive outings, and they offer a great way to meet people of a like mind.

PREPARATION

This is not your typical travel guide. The main emphasis is on individual extreme adventures, as the name suggests. In researching and writing this book the author and his assistants have purposely omitted listing mundane items that clog up most ordinary travel guides. Gone are restaurant reviews, tours from a car and hotel and motel listings. We feel you can figure these things out for yourself and would prefer we stick to the good stuff. We also assume you are traveling on a low budget (as we were). Therefore, the only accommodation listings you will find in *Extreme Adventures* are exceptional Youth Hostels and campground information.

Preparing for extended outings is, again, something the reader will have to figure out for himself/herself. If you can't pack, shop and prepare for a camping trip, you really shouldn't be going. The adventures in this book usually require equipment. When in doubt about something, ask an expert, such as the manager of a training, retail or rental shop.

The maps you will find in *Extreme Adventures* are designed to give you a geographical overview. Most are not to exact proportions and should be used as a supplement to your atlas or regular road map. *Extreme Adventure* park maps are there only for reference. The best park maps you can get are at the front gates and Ranger Stations of the parks themselves. Specifically, ask for the trail maps.

Most of the activities listed in this book require a certain degree of physical stamina. Some necessitate skill and physical training. A few are downright dangerous and potentially life-threatening. If you ever have even the slightest uncertainty about any adventure, DO NOT DO IT. It is wiser to know your limitations and "Just Say No," than to sustain an injury. You are the master of your body and only you can decide what is right for you.

Lastly, have a clue. We've said it before and we'll say it again: Be respectful of the natural environment. There is nothing worse than a person who trashes what little is left of our preserves and natural habitats. When you have affinity with nature, you tend to see more, to receive more. Something to think about before repelling off a 300-foot cliff.

Transportation

GETTING TO THE ISLANDS

Unless you are fortunate enough to be on a boat sailing to the islands, flying is the only option. The Hawaiian Islands are serviced by a plethora of airline companies all competing for your business. Most flights land in Honolulu on Oahu, but an increasing number are flying direct from the mainland to the Big Island, Maui and Kauai. The best plan is to shop around for the absolutely lowest airfare, then take an inter-island flight on **Aloha Airlines**, ☎ 800-367-5250, or **Hawaiian Airlines,** ☎ 800-367-5320. The inter-island fares are all at a fixed price that is under $85. Some neighboring islands, like Maui, Lanai, and Molokai, offer daily inter-island ferry shuttles.

GROUND PLAN

Since the airlines allow persons to check in bicycles as an article of luggage (usually with a small charge), readers are encouraged to do so. Having a road bike or mountain bike on Hawaii is a big advantage. Bikes are quick, easy and reliable transportation, and are a great way to have extreme adventures. The ultra low-budget traveler has been known to land with board and bike plus two carry-on bags of clothes, then peddle straight out from the airport. The only problems with bike-only transportation are the long distances on the bigger islands, and the torrential downpours from time to time.

Short trips usually require a vehicle. Car rental companies at the airports can get you into anything from a 4WD all-terrain vehicle to a luxury sedan or an el-cheapo economy car. Rental agreements for most cars prohibit off-road driving to some of the best island destinations. Anyone staying in Hawaii longer than a month should just purchase a used vehicle advertised in the newspaper. Hitchhiking is easy, legal, and usually a lot of fun (that is, if you don't mind waiting for your rides to stop).

LEGEND

- Volcanoes
- Lava Flows
- Windsurfing
- Diving
- Sacred Native Place
- Surfing
- Forbidden Island
- Kayaking
- Horseback Riding
- Shipwreck
- Waterfall
- Coral Reefs
- Party Town

The Thrill of It!

As you make your way through the thrills and spills of this book, you'll see that each extreme adventure has been rated for the risk involved and the potential adrenaline rush it may produce. Use these ratings as a guide only, and always use your own judgement. If you don't feel comfortable, don't participate. If you feel the urge to experience life at its fullest, go for it (no screamers please!).

RISK

1-2   Novice-friendly

3-4   Might Break A Sweat

5-6   Pretty Intense

7-8   Potentially Life-threatening

9-10   Professionals Only

ADRENALINE

1-2	Kid Stuff	😊
3-4	Pretty Good Pump	
5-6	Natural High	
7-8	Extreme Challenge	
9-10	Absolute Hairball	

☎ **AREA CODE**

All islands use the 808 area code.

Kapaa Park   Hawi   Keokea Park

KOHALA
COAST

Waipio
Valley

WINDWARD

Spencer
Park
Waimea   Hono kaa   Hikiau Falls

Mauna Lani Bay   Puako
Kona Village

Kalopa

Laupahoehoe Park

HAMAKUA
COAST

Kolekole Park

Akaka
Falls

13,796   Mauna
Kea

Rainbow
Falls

Hilo

Honokohau

8271   Hualalai

Cave
Saddle   Road

South
Hilo
Kaumana
Caves

Kailua-
Kona
Keauhou

CRATERS

Pahoa

130

Isaac Hule
Mackenzie

Kealakekua
Captain Cook

13,677
Mauna
Loa

Hawaii
Volcanoes
N.P.

Puna
District

137

Kealakekua
Bay
Napoopoo
Kealia
City of
Refuge

Kalapana

Kilauea
Crater

Roads
Closed due
to lava flows

LEEWARD

Pahala

Waiohinu
Waohinu
Naalehu

Punaluu Park
Honuapo
Wittington Park

LEGEND

> = Airport
△ = Camping
⚏ = Waterfall
≡○≡ = Sacred Native Place
◪ = Scuba & Snorkeling
◊ = Surfing
⚐ = Skiing

Jean
©1998

South
Point

BIG
ISLAND

CRATERS REGION

> "Shortly, the crater came into view. I have seen Vesuvius since, but it was a mere toy, a child's volcano, a soup-kettle, compared to this. Mount Vesuvius is a shapely cone 3,600 feet high; it's crater an incerted cone only 300 feet deep, and not more than 1,000 feet in diameter, if as much as that; its fires meager, modest, docile. But here was a vast perpendicular, walled cellar, 900 feet deep in some places, 1,300 in others, level-floored, and 10 miles in circumference! Here was a young pit upon whose floor the armies of Russia could camp, and have room to spare." ~ Mark Twain on Kilauea Crater

Viewing an active volcano is one of the most profound experiences this planet has to offer. Volcanoes shock all the senses. Roars and hisses tantalize the ear, lava rocks have a unique feel, the strong smell of sulfur can literally be tasted, and the awesome beauty of flowing magma is a treasure to any eyeball. Visitors fortunate enough to experience an eruption will certainly remember it for a lifetime. Even those who visit Kilauea Crater on an off-day will not walk away disappointed. Hawaii Volcanoes National Park is an outdoor museum in volcanology, geology, ecology, meteorology, surreal scenery and desolate solitude.

The ancient Hawaiian fire-goddess Pele, whose name means "volcano," is believed to reside in the Craters Region. Pele has visited all of the islands in turn, beginning at the northwest end of the chain and staying awhile on each, before choosing Mauna Loa and Kilauea as her home. Pele really gets around. She spends much of her time visiting other islands in the Pacific, but whenever there is an eruption on the Big Island, you can be sure she is close at hand. According to legend, it is Pele who tends the fiery furnaces and hurls the flaming red lava out of the boiling depths.

Radical adventurers will not be disappointed with all there is to do in the Craters Region. First, take a ride over the Saddle Road extending between Mauna Kea and Mauna Loa. From here, there are access roads to both of the nearly 14,000-foot summits, as well as several hiking trails into the upcountry. Mauna Kea receives a substantial amount of snow every winter, enticing skiers and snowboarders to get up there and carve some turns. When the wind is right, hang gliders can make one of the longest descents on the planet from the top of Mauna Kea to the sea. Kilauea Crater is a sight to behold, and hiking trails weave in and around the smoldering lava pit. Several other trails lead to interesting cinder cones and lava formations within Volcanoes National Park, as well as up to Mauna Loa, the world's largest active volcano.

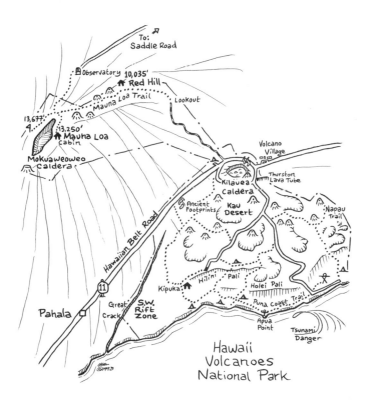

SADDLE ROAD

The first way to orients yourself with the Craters Region is to drive the Saddle Road. While the Big Island boasts 1,360 miles of highways (and not one freeway), the 55-mile Saddle Road is easily one of the most interesting sections. Rising 6,500 feet between two massive volcano cones and traversing an amazing spectrum of climatic zones, the Saddle Road is one of the most spectacular drives in all of Hawaii.

BIKING YOUR WAY ACROSS SADDLE ROAD

 RISK: 5   **ADRENALINE: 7**

Most coast roads are ideal for cycling, especially those around Waimea, but the most extreme bike excursion on the Big Island is crossing the Saddle Road. Leaving from Hilo, Saddle Road first passes through thick rainforest, then a fern forest until (around the 3,000-foot level) the landscape changes drastically to barren lava flows. In the middle of the "saddle" are turnoffs for both the Mauna Kea and Mauna Loa summits. If you have survived the bumps thus far, rejoice. Despite the fact that it took six hours riding time to reach the midpoint, it will take less than three hours to glide almost all the way down to the town of Waimea.

For a fun outfitter trip, sign up for a downhill ride with **Hawaiian Eyes** on their Mauna Kea Iki excursion. Participants get picked up early and descend 4,000 feet on the Observatory Road of Mauna Kea. No tough uphills and your lunch is included. What a deal!

TREKS STARTING FROM SADDLE ROAD

RISK: 2   ADRENALINE: 4

Five miles west of the Mauna Kea turnoff road is the lovely **Mauna Kea State Park**. It sits at 6,500 feet in the midst of rolling grasslands. This is base camp for multi-day hikes. You can pitch a tent or rent one of the seven cabins, which include hot showers and cooking utensils! Call for reservations as soon as possible. ☎ 808-961-7200.

From the park, it is possible to hike many miles of upcountry trails where you will probably not see another person. A two-mile hike from Mile Marker 35 brings you to a lookout offering a perfect view of the island's three largest volcanoes.

MAUNA KEA

No trip to the Big Island is complete without a visit to the top of towering Mauna Kea. Soaring to near stratospheric levels, Mauna Kea is a downright psychedelic place – so many observation domes on such a bleak landscape. The height and isolation make this summit one of the very best sites on earth for astronomical observations. Indeed, Mauna Kea is home to the world's foremost collection of optical and infrared telescopes.

The road is paved all the way to the top, but winter conditions and the steep downhill requires a 4WD vehicle. Apart from wandering around the dozen or so golf-ball-shaped observatories (no tours), don't miss **Lake Waiau**, just below the summit. Here is the highest lake in America on top of the highest mountain in the entire Pacific! On the way down from this frigid lunar landscape, stop at the 12,400-foot level. There is a marker for a short trail leading to **Keanakakoi**, "Cave of the Adzes," where ancient Hawaiians mined basalt for axe-like tools.

SNOWBOARDING
MAUNA KEA

 RISK: 3   ADRENALINE: 5

The ancient Hawaiians named Mauna Kea "white mountain" because of its snowy cap, which remains in place nearly half the year.

Scars on the mountain show that Mauna Kea was covered by glaciers during the last Ice Age – the only mountain in the central Pacific tall enough to have them. A winter wonderland!

The air is pretty thin up here, so if you're coming to ski, take your time getting acclimated. A 4WD vehicle will be necessary to haul you and your equipment up every run – sorry, no chairlifts. Powder conditions occur during the winter months after heavy rains in Hilo, but the base does not always receive that thick coating. Be prepared to thrash your boards. By doing so, you gain the bragging rights of having skied the world's highest tropical volcano!

HANG GLIDING
MAUNA KEA

RISK: 7   **ADRENALINE: 8**

Like its neighbor Mauna Loa 25 miles to the southwest, Mauna Kea is a shield volcano. That means most of its slope is very gentile, formed by many layers of lava resembling a warriors "shield." These gradual inclines, as well as a constant wind, are perfect for paragliding and hang gliding. While lower elevations (around the 6,000-foot level) offer more ideal takeoff conditions, some hot-doggers have launched from the 13,796-foot summit and glided all the way down to sea-level. This is America's highest takeoff-to-landing drop in elevation!

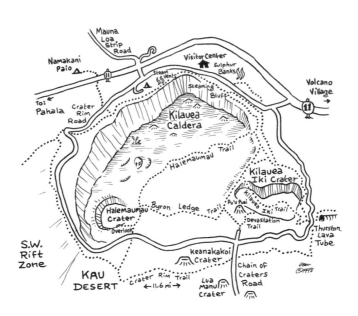

KILAUEA VOLCANO

Kilauea Volcano has been in a sustained eruption since 1983, when it woke up and started going ballistic. Lava continues to pour into the sea from fissures near Kilauea Caldera, most notably on the southeastern shore of **Hawaii Volcanoes National Park**. This ongoing eruption produces 14 million cubic feet of lava on a daily basis. As the lava flows downslope from the crater to the sea, it continues to build up and extend the shores of the Big Island. Since Kilauea's re-activation in 1983, the resulting lava flows have added 220 acres of new real estate to Hawaii. But before you go and buy your piece of paradise at "fire sale" prices, remember this land is extremely unstable. New ledges of lava extending out from the coastline continually break off when undercut by the sea. These sheered chunks tumble thousands of feet to the bottom of the ocean. Visitors to the national park must be aware of this hazard, and refrain from freestyle trail blazing. Stay only on marked trails and within the park's safety areas.

HIKES AROUND HAWAII VOLCANOES NATIONAL PARK

RISK: 3   ADRENALINE: 5

The first thing here is to do the 11-mile trip around Crater Rim Drive so you can take in the massive proportions of Kilauea. The next thing to do is park near the visitor's center and head for the **Halemaumau Trail**, which cuts straight through **Kilauea Crater**. Continue until you reach the crater overlook of the same name. Backtrack a half-mile to the **Byron Ledge Trail** for another walk along the crater floor. From here you can head back to the visitor's center, or take a mini-loop through another caldera – **Kilauea Iki Crater**.

Great barrenness is what you will find in the **Kau Desert**, even though it receives substantial rainfall. The reason it's so bleak is because natural gasses from Kilauea blend with the rain and produce a mixture too toxic for plants to grow. It is surreal to walk around the Kau Desert in the rain, which never really soaks into clothing because the heat from nearby lava flows make the rain evaporate almost upon impact. Trails for the Kau Desert start near Kilauea Crater, or on a trailhead beginning on Highway 11 about four miles south of the Mauna Loa Road. Near here is the **Footprints Trail**. Ancient footprints seen in the solidified ash were left by a band of warriors engulfed in a sudden eruption.

Another extreme hike in the park – the **Puna Coast Trail** – is in the southern section. Travel along desolate lava flows with the crashing ocean below your feet. Earthquakes off the coast sporadically produce tidal waves, which have wiped out large sections of this terrain. Collected rainwater is available at the three campground shelters, but be sure to bring plenty to spare. It gets hot out here. This is a multi-day excursion requiring you to register for a backcountry permit at the visitor's center.

LAVA TUBE SPELUNKING
RISK: 1   ADRENALINE: 2

Thurston Lava Tube is considered the most accessible lava tunnel because it's located just off Crater Rim Drive. Follow the throng of bus tourists to the fern jungle entrance. The tube is 450 feet long and 10 feet high, and pops out into another fern jungle on the other side. The most remarkable aspect of this tube is the smoothness of the walls. Roots dangle down from the ferns above. No need for a flashlight; it's well lit, albeit artificially. Parking here offers good access to Kilauea Iki Crater and its famous trail. You might also snake around via the Crater Rim Trail and visit the fascinating Devastation Trail.

ACTIVE VOLCANO TREKKING

RISK: 6

ADRENALINE: 9

Hiking over lava flows on unmarked trails is seriously frowned upon by Park Rangers. They will tell you the only way you can see active lava is if it happens to be flowing right by the road.

Should you wish to break the rules and go trekking at your own risk, we recommend the Chain of Craters Road. It is officially closed after a certain point, and the Rangers will tell you to turn back, but if you happen to arrive on a lucky lava day (the lava is not always flowing), you'll be missing out if you don't keep on going. Leave your car at the road's end and continue on foot.

Up on higher ground a fissure is spewing large quantities of lava. As you wander onto uncharted territory, look for the plumes of smoke near the ocean. This is where the lava makes contact with the sea.

MAUNA LOA VOLCANO

Although presently quiet, Mauna Loa, the world's largest active volcano, could erupt again at any time. According to scientists, another eruption on Mauna Loa is long overdue, but could still be several years away. Accurately predicting eruptions is not easy. Earthquakes and seismic activity are the major tip-offs, as are swelling and inflation of the land, which suggest magma rising from within. Fotrunately, none of this is happening around Mauna Loa now.

Mauna Loa has erupted 33 times in the last 150 years, yet only the 1975 and 1984 eruptions have been studied carefully by scientists. During the harrowing 1984 event, lava flows stopped a mere eight miles short of downtown Hilo.

THREE-DAY TREK TO THE SUMMIT

RISK: 3

ADRENALINE: 6

The opportunity exists to climb the world's largest active volcano – over 10,000 cubic miles of mountain. As previously mentioned, Mauna Loa last erupted in 1984 and could possibly erupt again within the next few years. Thus, there is a popular saying: "He who has the chance to climb it once and doesn't, is a fool. He who has the chance to climb it twice and does, is the same."

First-timers start at the visitor's center near Kilauea and allow three or four days to hike the summit and back. Lucky lottery winners can use one of two cabins along their trek, or else camp in the wilderness on the lava rocks (see page 33 for details on lottery drawings). The Mauna Loa Road (which may be driven) from the visitor's center rises along the "Long Mountain" in a gentle fashion, ending at a 6,662-foot lookout after 13.5 miles. After the lookout the **Mauna Loa Trail** begins, extending 7.5 miles to the Red Hill Cabin. The next day's hike continues past several cinder cones for 9.5 miles to the Mokuaweoweo Caldera. At this point, the trail forks. It is about two miles around the deep caldera to the Mauna Loa Cabin at 13,250 feet, or to the summit at 13,677 feet. The panorama of Hawaii volcanoes and Maui island from the top is absolutely spectacular. This is not a technical climb, but suited only to those with strong lungs and legs and healthy hearts.

LOiHi VOLCANO

Extreme adventurers will have to wait a while on this one. The newest Hawaiian Island is still 3,200 feet below the ocean surface. Loihi, an undersea volcano, lies 21 miles southeast of the Big Island, and is actively rumbling over Hawaii's Hot Spot. It is not predicted to break the surface of the water for at least another hundred years, maybe another 10,000 years, but recent earthquakes have prompted University of Hawaii scientists to study it carefully. They even sent a mini-submarine down to check it out. They found much silt in the water, indicating movement, and a considerable change to Loihi's previously charted landscape.

Eruption patterns on Loihi are believed to be much like those on the Big Island – sustained eruptions with intense intervals of activity. In a two-week period during the summer of 1996, Loihi produced 4,070 measurable earthquakes; 95 of the quakes measured 4.0 or larger on the Richter scale, and the largest detected was a 5.0 magnitude. Scientists fear another series of larger quakes, generated by eruptions of Loihi or movement of its flank, could cause locally generated tidal waves (*tsunamis*).

Outfitters & Resources

Dept. of Land and Natural Resources
Division of State Parks
PO Box 936 (75 Aupuni St.)
Hilo, HI 96720
☎ 808-961-7200
*Cabin/camping permits for all Big Island
state parks.*

Hawaiian Eyes, Big Island Bicycle Tours
PO Box 1500
Honokaa, HI 96727
☎ 808-885-8806
*Half-day and full-day bike excursions down
the upper slopes of Mauna Kea.*

Mauna Kea Beach Hotel
62-100 Mauna Kea Beach Drive
Kamuela, HI 96743
☎ 808-882-7222
*This hotel has an arrangement with Parker
Ranch to conduct horseback tours across
the quarter-million acres of open range on
the slopes of Mauna Kea.*

Ski Guides Hawaii
PO Box 2020
Kamuela, HI 96743
☎ 808-889-6747
When the snow falls, from December through May, these guys provide ski and snowboard rentals, as well as lifts to the top of Mauna Kea.

Volcano Helitours
Volcano Golf and Country Club
Mile Marker 30, PO Box 626
Kilauea Volcano, HI 96785
☎ 808-967-7578
Little time is wasted with the heliport so close to the active volcanoes.

4WD RENTAL COMPANIES
Harper, ☎ 808-969-1478
Ciao Exoticar, ☎ 808-326-2426
4WD vehicles necessary for Mauna Kea and other Big Island radical excursions.

Leeward Side

"The same coast on which the far-voyager Cook ended a noble career not so nobly. That district of Kona where he fell is one illustrious in the history of Hawaii. It was at first the center of the dominion of the great Kamehameha." ~ Robert Lewis Stevenson, *Travels in Hawaii*, 1889

The arrival of Captain James Cook in 1778 began an era of incredible change – for not only the native Hawaiians, but for the land itself. Those who followed in Cook's wake – the explorers, missionaries, and merchants – brought a new world of possessions, ideas, religions, customs, and diseases to these once-isolated islands. The different plants and animals that came with each new group made devastating inroads on indigenous species, causing many extinctions and near-extinctions, particularly among endemic birds. Before an understanding of this new paradigm could be formulated, the old ways of the Hawaiians had already been changed forever.

The **Kona Coast**, literally meaning the "Leeward Side," is steeped in ancient Hawaiian tradition and historical landmarks. Here the extreme adventurer can take a journey back in time and discover well-preserved petroglyphs, *heiaus* (temples), King Kamehameha's Royal Palace, and Pu'uhonua O Honaunau – popularly known as the City of Refuge. Not far away is Kealakekua Bay, where Captain Cook met his undignified fate. A monument stands to commemorate where the great navigator fell.

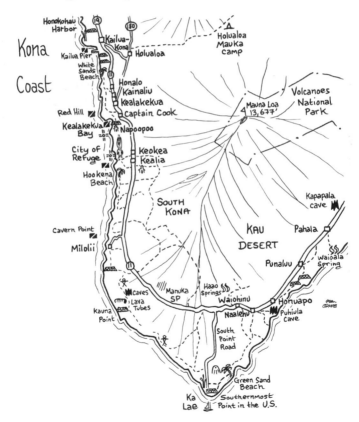

Best of all, the leeward side means fun in the sun. Here you will enjoy beautiful sun-filled days all year round, as well as some of the finest beaches on the Big Island. This also means you will find a large concentration of hotels and tourists. Because the leeward side is shielded from the wet trade winds, the coastal water is calm, with little runoff, thus providing ideal diving conditions. The sheltered coves also offers a rare opportunity to swim with dolphins in the open sea. Or you can take a charter out to thousand-foot-deep waters and try your luck at some deep-sea fishing.

EXCELLENT DIVING

Diving on the leeward side of the Big Island is considered some of the best in the whole state of Hawaii. Calm and clear conditions year-round, as well as ocean surface temperatures of 73° in the winter and 80° in the summer, make the Kona Coast ideal for snorkelers and scuba divers alike. The island's soaring volcanoes provide protection from rain and wind and, because there is so little runoff, coral flourishes and visibility is typically in the 100-foot range. Since the Big Island is so new geologically, the diver can expect dramatic drop-offs close to shore, a wide variety of deep-water and inshore reef animals, as well as a honeycomb of caves, arches, tunnels and lava tubes. Here are some of the most notable sites:

CAVERN POINT LAVA TUBES

RISK: 6

ADRENALINE: 5

Cavern Point is renowned as the most extensive underwater lava tube system discovered in Hawaii to date. Dive lights are necessary when exploring the interior of these tubes because no light, other than from the entrance, can penetrate. It's a good idea to bring a back-up light as well. The floors of the tubes are compiled of small rocks, not sand and silt, so don't worry about stirring up sediment and losing your way. Cavern Point is usually done as two separate dives – Twin Lava Tubes and Three Room Cave. Both are located just north of Laeokamimi Point in South Kona.

Twin Lava Tubes provides just what its name suggests: two 15-foot-diameter tubes penetrating over 150 feet into the sheer lava-rock face. The tubes are stacked one on top of the other, with a small connection in the middle. To add excitement, the walls are scored with cracks housing shrimp, lobster, and other sea critters, as well as air chambers inside the upper tube. **Three Room Cave** is an amazing complex of high vaulted ceilings connecting a maze of tubes and caverns.

"Swiss Cheese" would be a more appropriate name because there are far more than three rooms here. Both dives are accessible only by a South Kona boat operator (see *Outfitters & Resources,* below) and both are at about 50 feet below the surface.

CITY OF REFUGE SHORE DIVE

 RISK: 4   ADRENALINE: 4

Snorkelers usually access this dive straight from the beach; divers more typically suit-up on the lava shelf and use the natural steps for easy entry. Either way, once your mask is in the water, you are greeted with one of the most abundant tropical fish zones on the leeward side. Indeed, this whole region is protected. Several parallel reefs jut outward and offer a multitude of color and life. Farther out, near the mouth of the bay, a sheer face drops quickly to 160 feet. Those who enjoy wall dives can head out here. Those that seek caves should go to the north side of the bay. Almost everyone spots a sea turtle or two, as well as eels, crabs and a variety of shells.

KAILUA AREA DIVES

RISK: 4   ADRENALINE: 4

Just to the north and south of Kailua town are several excellent dive spots accessible by boat and from shore. **Red Hill** is eight miles south of town and features red lava formations and many caves. It is accessible only by boat. **Kailua Pier** offers easy shore entry and is quite popular for night diving. **Old Airport** is another popular shore dive, with lots of aquatic life, archways, caves, and even a blowhole which can be explored on calm days. The south end of Old Airport is especially favored at night when the lights are on at the adjacent tennis courts and baseball field, providing illumination.

Abundant marine life keeps divers coming back for more.

Kaiwi Point, just to the north of Kailua, is an excellent dive site close to shore. Kaiwi Point a good night dive, with large caves, their ceilings covered with bright orange cup coral. A little farther north is **Keahole Point**, where divers can enter the cockpit of a sunken airplane. And last but not least is **Pine Trees**, a series of several spectacular dives: Carpenter's House, Golden Arches, and Pinnacle Peak, all at 30-100-foot depths and accessible by boat only.

★

KOHALA COAST DIVES
RISK: 4   ADRENALINE: 4

Pukako is a small cove just off Pukako Beach Road, about 30 miles north of Kailua. Pukako offers pretty easy shore access into some of the most consistent 100-foot-visibility waters on the leeward coast. Snorkelers who can hold their breath may swim down 10 feet and see the entrance to a long lava tube. Scuba divers may enter this tube and pass through to the 30-foot depths on the ocean side. To locate the shallow-side entrance, swim through the cove about 150 feet, turn to the north (right), and look for three deep vertical shafts in the lava shelf.

WARNING...

Currents are very strong on the outer portion of the reef at Pukako, where the depth exceeds 100 feet.

Photographers will enjoy the shallow caves and colorful coral at the **Pentagon**, where the depths do not exceed 35 feet. Five massive openings connect the "Pentagon," which then connect and interweave into a complex of other tunnels and archways. The Pentagon is only 1,500 feet off the beautiful Waikoloa Beach, however most divers opt to take a boat.

Another outstanding boat excursion is to **Horseshoe Cove** in the northern portion of the Kohala Coast. Boats anchor at a mooring near the mouth of the cove, and divers are greeted with a large overhang at 45 feet, leading to a spectacular lava tube. Take the left fork inside the tube and follow it to an exit, which pops out at an 80-foot depth. From here, follow the extension of an underwater ridge to the surface. Parallel to the sloping ridge lies another lava tube at 25 foot. This tube is known for all its "windows," which allow sunlight to beam through, as well as the dome at the end (it also has several openings). No need to go any farther than Horseshoe Cove for a second dive. On the south side and inside walls of the horseshoe there is a seemingly endless array of tunnels stretching along the reef. Horseshoe Bay is also renowned for housing one of the most diverse and widest displays of aquatic life in Hawaii.

```
WARNING...
Do not dive Horseshoe Bay when
the ocean is rough. The lava
tubes fill with surges and silt
up, making it dangerous.
```

KOHALA COAST ADVENTURES

One of the best road bicycle rides is from Waimea to Hawi along the naturally cool **Kohala Mountain Road**. This very scenic route reaches an elevation of 3,500 feet and allows views of all three Big Island volcanoes, as well as the shimmering ocean below. Looping around on the north Kohala Coast are excellent beaches and trails leading to ancient *heiaus,* petroglyphs, and the paved King's Trail near the town of Puako. Farther south, it is possible to hike up 8,271-foot Mount Hualalai via the Hualalai Trail near the town of Holualoa. This is the beginning of the Kona coffee-growing district, and hiking, horseback riding and mountain biking trails abound. Check with a local for open routes.

IRONMAN TRIATHLON
RISK: 6   ADRENALINE: 8

Perhaps the most grueling triathlon competition on earth is held on the leeward side of the Big Island in the middle of October every year. The superhuman participants undergo an amazing amount of exercise in one single day. First, a 2.4-mile ocean swim across Kailua Bay, then a 112-mile bicycle ride, and, finally, a full 26-mile marathon run. Just to say you completed the Ironman is worthy of lifelong bragging rights, let alone proof you are one in-shape dude (or dudette). Contact ☎ 808-329-0063 for applications and more information.

DEEP-SEA FISHING

Fishing has been an integral part of native Hawaiian life since people first arrived 1,800 years ago. The ancients mostly fished with round nets edged with weights. They would scan the waters with a keen eye for big fishes, then cast out the net. Another technique involved going into the shallows at night with a torch and spear. The fish were attracted to the lights at night, and fishermen would take aim and attempt to spear the biggest fish they could. Both of these techniques are still practiced, but when most people think about fishing on the Kona Coast, they think of deep-sea fishing. The Kona Coast is considered to have the best marlin waters in all the oceans of the world. Many boats here charter tours, and the lucky ones are equipped with a fish-god on deck. The marlin record holder, a tourist who hauled in a 796-pound fish, attributed his good fortune to the commonly-seen fish-god memento on his charter craft. Something to think about when considering boats.

DEEP-SEA FISHING OFF THE KONA COAST

 RISK: 4 **ADRENALINE: 2**

Marlin are not the only thing fishermen hope take to their lines. Sailfish, aku, ahi, barracuda, bonito, mahimahi, ono, ulua and tuna disport themselves in the deep off-shore waters. Because the Big Island is so new geologically, the drop-off begins only a short way from the shore. Boats needn't travel far to get to where the big boys reside. (See *Outfitters & Resources*, below.)

CITY OF REFUGE EXCURSION

Pu'uhonua O Honaunau, popularly known as the City of Refuge, is the single most evocative historical site in all the Hawaiian Islands. The **Pu'uhonua O Honaunau National Historic Park** has been completely restored and preserved precisely the way it appeared to Captain Cook and his men in the late 1700's. Reach the park along the bumpy coastal road, four miles south from Kealakekua Bay. Entrance to the park is $1 per person, and it's open daily from 7:30 am until midnight.

The function of a *Pu'uhonua* was to absolve the guilty. Every island in Hawaii had at least one of these forgiving gods. The deal was that a convicted criminal, defeated warrior, or pacifist wishing to wait out a conflict could come here and receive instant immunity and absolution from any previous entanglement, no matter what the circumstance. However, the difficult part was simply *getting here*. After a guilty verdict, a convicted criminal was set loose to reach a life-saving *Pu'uhonua*, or face the wrath of the accuser or *kapu* of vengeful gods. War parties set out after the criminal by land, while hostile canoeists and sharks created obstacles by sea. Even when the criminal got close to a *Pu'uhonua* complex, he still had to get past a strongly guarded royal enclave. Once inside the *Pu'uhonua*, the criminal would go through a cleansing ritual lasting only a few hours, then walk out free to resume a normal life.

FULL MOON AT THE CITY OF REFUGE

 RISK: 2   ADRENALINE: 3

Perhaps the best way to experience Pu'uhonua O Honaunau is on the night of a full moon. Discover this place for the first time on an illuminated night when there are few tourists around. Check out the restored remains of the royal palace, including a fish pond, the beach and private canoe landing, and the three sacred *heiaus,* all guarded by bizarre effigies of pissed-off Hawaiian gods. Best of all is the massive Great Wall enclosure. Its masonry was constructed in the 16th century, without use of mortar. Pop a mushy cap and off you go!

KEALAKEKUA BAY

Captain Cook was first received on the Big island by thousands of natives who threw themselves at his feet, believing him to be their long-lost god Lono. Cook and his crew (one of whom was Lieutenant Bligh, later famous as the captain of *The Bounty*) were given a royal Hawaiian reception and all the supplies they requested. Trouble began when Cook returned to Kealakekua Bay a second time, only a few weeks later. The Hawaiians thought him and his men to be freeloading, and stole a small boat as compensation one night. Cook went ashore to get his boat back and a skirmish broke out. Soon Cook was dead, lying face down in a foot of water. The young warrior Kamehameha was present at Cook's death and some say he made the final death blow. Other reports say he merely cut off some of Cook's hair.

Kamehameha was a fierce warrior and cunning general. Standing over six and a half feet tall and weighing 300+ pounds, his mere presence would strike fear into any opponent. History shows Kamehameha became the first king to unify the Big Island, then went on to dominate them all. He ruled justly and wisely until his death in 1819, and gave the islands strength and unity in the face of increasing foreign influence. Kamehameha's burial site is unknown, but the most probable location is within the sacred caves high above the steep cliffs surrounding Kealakekua Bay. It's quite possible Captain Cook is buried there as well.

PILGRIMAGE TO GREAT LEADERS

 RISK: 1 **ADRENALINE: 2**

The only way to get down the narrow track to Kealakekua ("Road of the God") Bay is by hiking or on horseback. Pay close attention to the sheer cliff walls; this is the final resting place of many prominent Hawaiian chiefs. Most of these ancient burial caves have never been opened, and probably never will be. At the bottom of the road is Napoopoo, a former fishing village and location of many ruined *heiaus*. Follow the coastal trail to the north end of the bay where you will find a white obelisk. This is the Captain Cook Monument, commemorating the actual spot where the great navigator breathed his last. There is great diving just off shore.

WARNING...

Avoid swimming in the early evening, when sharks come in to feed.

DOLPHIN SWIM ON KONA COAST

Dolphins are highly evolved and intelligent beings. There are many documented cases of dolphins risking their own lives to save people from drowning, thus proving their unconditional love and compassion for the human race. Dolphin brains are as large as humans, yet researchers believe dolphins have the capacity to use nearly 100% of their brain, whereas humans use a mere 10% of theirs. Dolphins communicate via sound waves, or echolocation, which can create feelings of entering a deep meditative and healing state in humans. But their communication has much more to teach us. Leading researchers believe dolphins pass on an oral tradition to their young similar to that of human tribal nations. Dolphins may well know what has been going on around this planet for the last 25 million years and could someday translate this consciousness to us landlubbers.

Dolphins, like humans, are very family-oriented. They swim in family units and can travel up to 100 miles per day. While we have much to learn from dolphins, *Extreme Adventures* can't endorse the popular Kona hotel dolphin swims. Dolphins are accustomed to swimming in much larger areas – not "pools." One operator on the Big Island (Dolphin Discovery Tours, listed on page 54) uses open habitats where the dolphins can come and go as they please.

Instructors at Dolphin Discovery Tours explain how dolphins give birth, swim and breathe.

DOLPHIN SWIM IN
KEALAKEKUA BAY

 RISK: 2   ADRENALINE: 7

A much better alternative for interacting with dolphins is in the wild, on their terms. One of the best places to snorkel on the Kona Coast is Kealakekua Bay. Not only is the aquatic life amazing here, but this is a common playing ground of spinner dolphins.

Kealakekua Bay is an underwater state park and marine preserve; perhaps the dolphins sense this and come here knowing they won't be harmed. Many boat charters make trips out here hoping to encounter schools of dolphins.

SOUTH POINT BLOW HOLE TREK

The southernmost section of the Big Island is known as the **Kau District**, named after the Kau Desert on Kilauea's barren southwestern slope. **Mauna Loa's** slope rises to the north, its vegetation sparse and scrubby. Off the Belt Road, a side road to South Point takes you to a lighthouse at the southernmost tip of the Hawaiian Islands. This is **Ka Lae**, which is also the southernmost point of the United States and an extremely windy location due to the prevailing trade winds. This was a sacred area to ancient Hawaiians. Several trails lead to *heiaus*, petroglyphs, ancient canoe moorings and a blowhole.

TRIP TO
GREEN SANDS BEACH

 RISK: 2   ADRENALINE: 2

From the Kaulana Boat Ramp at South Point, it's two miles northeast over a rough rutted track to the famous Green Sands Beach. Hike, mountain-bike, or take a 4WD vehicle to the base of **Puu Mahana** cinder cone, where you will find a trail down to the beach. The greenish tint of the sand is caused by a mineral called olivine, which has eroded from the cinder hill rising above the beach. Hiking round-trip takes about two hours.

Outfitters & Resources

Big Island Divers
Honokohau Harbor
☎ 808-329-6068
Low cost certification course for locals. Also provides rentals and excursions.

Captain Zodiac Cruises
Honokohau Yacht Harbor
☎ 808-329-3199
Adventure rafting. Humpback whale tours, snorkeling trips and dolphin swims (all three if you're lucky).

Dolphin Discovery Tours
PO Box 9901
Waimanalo, HI 96795
☎ 800-888-3657 or 808-259-8530
Runs guided trips to swim with the dolphins in Kealakekua Bay.

Jack's Diving Locker
Kona Inn Shopping Village
☎ 808-329-7585 or 800-345-4807
Over 50 diving and snorkeling excursions along the Kona coast. Sales, rentals and certification coiurses available.

Kenai Helicopters
Mile Marker 75 along Route 19
Waikaloa Village, north of Kailua-Kona
☎ 808-329-7424 or 800-622-3144
One of the oldest and most knowledgeable operators. Try their "Fire and Rain Tour."

King Kamehameha Divers
King Kamehameha Kona Beach Hotel
Kailua-Kona, HI 96745
☎ 808-329-5662
Daily scuba and snorkeling trips along the Kona Coast. Equipment and meals provided.

King's Trail Rides
Highway 11, just outside Kealakekua
☎ 808-323-2388
Horseback ride and lunch on the real working Kealakekua ranch. Buses take you to Ranch HQ and stables at 4,200-foot elevation.

Kohala Divers
Route 270, Kawaihae Shopping Center
Kawaihae, HI 96743
☎ 808-882-7774
The only dive company on the Kohala Coast. Accesses some great locations. Rentals and certification available.

Kona Kai Diving
PO Box 4178
Kailua-Kona, HI 96745
☎ 808-329-0695

Another fine dive charter company, this one specializes in natural and cultural history between dives.

Kona Marlin Center
Honokohau Harbor
☎ 808-329-7529 or 800-648-7529
These are the old pros at catching the "big blue" marlin.

Kona Water Sports
☎ 808-329-1593
Conducts parasailing and waterskiing excursions. They also rent Jet Skis.

DEEP-SEA FISHING CHARTERS
Aloha Charter Fishing and Activities
☎ 808-329-2200
Kona Coast Activities
☎ 808-329-3171
Marlin Country Charters
☎ 808-326-1666
Omega Sport Fishing
☎ 808-325-7859
Pamela Big Game Fishing
☎ 808-329-1525
Roy Gay
☎ 808-329-6041
Seawife Charters
☎ 808-329-1806
Twin Charter Sportfishing
☎ 808-329-4753

Windward Side

"In what other land save this one is the commonest form of greeting not 'Good Day,' ... but 'Love?' ... It is the positive affirmation of one's own heart giving." ~ Jack London, 1916

The windward coast of the Big Island of Hawaii is known by many names. Last century so many Scots worked the sugarcane plantations that the coast was known as the "Scotch Coast." Hawaiians refer to this wet stretch of land as the "Hamakua Coast," south of Hilo is the "South Hamakua Coast," and when the prominent east coast hooks southward around Kapoho Point, you have the "Puna District." For simplicity's sake, we'll just refer to the whole area as the windward coast of the Big Island, named for the dominating weather pattern which keeps this side rather wet and tropical.

The town of **Hilo**, the state's most tropical city, is right in the middle of the windward coast and a good starting point for exploring the area. Hilo miraculously survived not only one, but two enormous tidal waves in 1946 and 1960. Perhaps being wiped off the map twice in 14 years is what makes the town appear seedy, but the people sure are friendly. Wandering around town it's easy to see how the Big Island earned the name "The Orchid Island." Botanical gardens and flower farms surround Hilo like a giant lei. This is one of the oldest settlements in Hawaii, and also one of the wettest: 133 inches of (mostly winter) rain drench Hilo every year. For this reason, most tourists stay on the mega-sunny leeward side, which makes Hilo affordable and pretty low key. In addition, Jack London would be glad to know the "Aloha Spirit" is alive and well in Hilo.

Any tour of the windward coast begins, and ends, along Route 19 north of Hilo to Waipio Valley, and Route 11 south of Hilo to Puna. Both roads are collectively known as the Belt Road. This is your access point to *extreme adventures* along the windward coast. Hitching is pretty easy if you can't afford a rental car, but the wait time eats up valuable play time. Mountain bikes are ideal on the access and old sugarcane roads, yet not too practical on the vast distances of the Big Island. The best vehicle is a 4WD jeep, perfect for getting just about anywhere. Hilo is also the starting point for the super-scenic Saddle Road (see *Craters Region*, page 20). The best time for windward adventures is the often-sunny mornings.

To: Hilo
Keaau
Puna Trail
Honolulu Boat Landing
Mountain View
130
Cape Kumukahi
Lava Tree S.P.
Pahoa
132
137
Kamiaili Pit Crater
Pohoiki
Hot Springs
Isaac Hale Beach
PUNA DISTRICT
Opihikao
MacKenzie State Park
Kilauea Caldera
Kehana
Active Flows
Ancient Paved Trail
Volcanoes National Park
Kalapana
Kaimu Black Sands Beach
Road closed
Puu Loa
21 Miles away
3,200 feet down
Loihi Seamount

WAIPIO VALLEY

Waipio Valley is the largest and longest valley on the Big Island. Six miles deep and a mile wide at the mouth, this verdant valley is surrounded by 2,000-foot *pali* (cliffs) sheering nearly straight up. Getting down into the valley is quite a challenge along a steep, one-mile road descending from the lookout. Only four-wheel-drive vehicles, donkey riders or hikers can make it down. The valley floor is checkered with abandoned taro patches, and constantly watered by several waterfalls in the valley. Hawaii's highest cascade,

Hiilawe Waterfall, tumbles 1,300 feet at the rear of the valley.

King Kamehameha the Great spent much of his boyhood in Waipio Valley and returned many times during his adulthood. Many great kings were buried here, and it was in this valley that Kamehameha came to renew his spiritual power. Legend has it that the great king hid out in Waipio during his adolescence so the other chiefs could not subjugate him. He waited, amassed his prophesied power, and went on to become the first and only king to unify all the Hawaiian islands.

TRIBAL RUN THROUGH WAIPIO VALLEY

 RISK: 2   ADRENALINE: 3

 In honor of King Kamehameha and all the great rulers buried in this "Valley of Kings," we ask that you play along a little on this one. Today you are a tribal member of Kamehamea's court. Back then it was mostly royalty, priests, warriors, and high-ranking officials who occupied the sacred Waipio Valley. The remains of four *heiaus*, or Hawaiian temples, lie in the valley. Unfortunately, all the *heiaus* today are merely piles of volcanic rocks after being slammed by a giant tidal wave in 1946, but don't let that stop you. The *heiaus* still

contain the spirit of Royal Hawaii and were once used to make sacrifices to the gods – sometimes human.

Imagine this is a day of intense energy. The king has summoned a war party, and all warriors are to report at the giant *heiau* near the beach. The sounds of drums and conch shells echo frequently off the valley walls. You are up the stream where thousands of villagers once lived. Time to run! Along the stream banks, run until you reach the black sand beach. Turn right and continue running all the way down to the beach's end. On the right-hand side of the beach as you face the sea is the *Paka'alana Heiau* in a grove of trees. Go to it, your friends are warriors with you. Meditate on this spot and try to visualize an immense war party setting out to sea. Kamehameha is at the stern of the largest boat looking regal and powerful. Acknowledge his presence. In Waipio Valley, you might just get a reply.

WAIMANU VALLEY TREK

For those seeking the true C.O.R.E. (Comrades Of Radical Excursions) experience while in the Waipio Valley region, there is no better excursion than the 11-mile trek from Waipio to Waimanu Valley. This is one of the most difficult hikes in the whole state of Hawaii. But the effort is well worth it — once there, it is an untouched paradise on earth. Waimanu Valley is best described as a miniature version of Waipio, only with no permanent settlements and more waterfalls.

CAMPING TREK TO WAIMANU VALLEY

 RISK: 7 ADRENALINE: 8

 The trailhead to Waimanu begins in Waipio Valley at the far end of the beach, slightly inland. After battling the steep uphill to the top, the trail weaves in and out of a succession of untamed gullies, never touching sea level until you reach Waimanu Valley. Even in Waimanu, the beach consists of large boulders, unsuitable for ocean adventures. The joy of this trip is experiencing the untamed Hawaiian jungle. Along the way, trekking parties will have to wade through at least two deep and fast-flowing streams Indiana Jones-style. For this reason, the trail is passable only in the summer, from May until October.

This hike simply can't be done in one day. Trekkers must be prepared to walk and camp in rainy conditions. It is imperative to bring everything necessary for a backcountry expedition: most important are a rainproof jacket and tent, sturdy shoes, and a water purification system. Trekkers to Waimanu are also required to obtain a free camping permit (Dept. of Forestry, 1643 Kilauea Ave., Hilo HI 96720; ☎ 933-4221).

HORSEBACK RIDING

The northern section of the windward coast offers ample opportunities to ride horses on a working ranch, or venture deep into the jungle. Experienced guides take riders on horseback excursions through the spectacular Waipio Valley, clip-clopping past waterfalls, taro patches and spiritual spots. It takes only half an hour to get down the steep trail, so most of the time on the Waipio excursion is spent touring the valley. Another popular place to ride horses is **Kalopa State Recreation Area**, which has a horseback loop through the jungle. Contact one of the outfitters listed at the end of this chapter for more information.

WORKING RANCH RIDES
RISK: 2   ADRENALINE: 3

Real horseback riders will appreciate real horses used on a real working ranch among real beautiful settings. These are not your typical tourist horses that don't run. On the contrary, these horses are used by the Hawaiian cowboys (*paniolos*), and are thus quite strong beasts of burden. Walk, trot or canter your horse through lush pastureland with breathtaking views all around. Stops include a native *ohia* grove and the ruins of an ancient Hawaiian village. Contact **Paniolo Riding Adventures** at ☎ 808-889-5354 to make your reservation.

HAMAKUA COAST

The former sugarcane coast is often overlooked by excited travelers trying to get to or from Waipio Valley and Hilo. Big mistake. Hurry past here and you'll miss beautiful gorges and valleys, little-known forest preserves, scenic tropical landscapes, and quaint one-street villages seemingly lost in time. This is the Big Island preserved in an age when time didn't seem to move so fast. Best is to discover the Hamakua Coast at random. Pull off at a little town and ask a local where he goes for his extreme adventures. Chances are you'll get directions to a place not mentioned in any travel book.

 ## AKAKA FALLS GULCH
RISK: 2 ADRENALINE: 2

One of the major rewards of the 50-mile Hamakua Coast is the spectacular drive itself, which offers mile after mile of intense tropical beauty. One of the most popular turnoffs leads to **Akaka Falls State Park**, which is three or four miles up Mauna Kea from the belt road, and 15 miles out of Hilo. The 66-acre park is in a jungle-like gorge and has several stunning waterfalls, prime territory for a Tarzan experience. The flora is so thick overhead that the light has an eerie, dusk-like quality. Catch a vine and off you go.

HILO AREA ADVENTURES

Hilo averages an astonishing 130 inches of rainfall annually. The reason why tourism never took off in Hilo is simply because it rains too much. "America's Wettest City" is usually clear and radiant in the mornings, but, like clockwork, the clouds and rain move in after lunch. Kauai may be the "Garden Island," but over 2,500 species of plants and flowers flourish on the Big Island's landscape, 95% found only in Hawaii. All this precipitation and vegetation spells major tropical jungle adventures.

RAINBOW FALLS & BOILING POTS

RISK: 3   **ADRENALINE: 2**

Rainbow Falls is quite easy to find. Just head on up Waianuenue Avenue two miles and turn on Rainbow Drive. Get here early to see rainbows form in the morning mist. The extreme adventure is getting down a very muddy and slippery staircase to stream level. Here you can freestyle over the rocks for a swim in the pool, or just marvel at the astonishing view of the falls with looming Mauna Kea as a backdrop. The Boiling Pots are one more mile up the road; signs indicate the turnoff. The Boiling Pots are springs of water percolating up from the lava beds. A crude path to the right gets you an up-close view of the pots, as well as a few more falls and pools.

KAUMANA CAVES

RISK: 3   ADRENALINE: 4

Two miles past Rainbow Falls, the Saddle Road splits off to the left. Most drivers turn inland at the route 200 sign off Highway 19 just north of Hilo. On the road up the mountain is Kaumana Caves for your exploration pleasures. Bring your camera for a picture-perfect cave entrance shot in the midst of a beautiful fern grotto. The cave is a lava tube which ranges from three to 15 feet high and 10 to 60 feet wide. It can be followed for more than half a mile. This tube was formed in the 1881 flow, which lasted for nine months and came closer to Hilo than any flow on record. Flashlights required.

PUNA COAST ADVENTURES

The main town in Puna, **Pahoa**, has become a gathering place for alternative lifestylers and latter-day hippies. New Agers have congregated here with their funky shops, whole food restaurants, and liberal views (read: good place to find ganja). Six miles away on the coast, snorkeling is pretty interesting in the tidepools, but the open seas are a bit too rough. The best stop is **Isaac Hale Beach Park** in picturesque

Pohoiki Bay, popular with surfers, fishermen and hikers. Unfortunately, most of Puna's best beaches have been wiped out by recent lava flows. Where the road ends may be a good place to see an active lava flow. This all depends on which way the lava is flowing on any given day. For more information on exploring lava flows, see the *Craters Region*, page 28.

KALAPANA BLACK SAND BEACH

This is the raw coast of Hawaii: new, violent and spectacular. This is how the islands must have looked before a living soul ever set foot upon them. Volcanic boulders from nearby Kilauea have been shattered by the sea and ground into the black sands of Kalapana. The surf foaming along the edges of dark sand and the grove of swaying palms rustling against the sky create a vision of paradise all too rare in the world today.

ROBINSON CRUSOE FANTASY

 RISK: 3   ADRENALINE: 2

Almost all the village of Kalapana has been destroyed by recent eruptions. With danger in the air and not another village for many miles, this is secluded Hawaii at its best. So far away from it all, it's easy to find a remote beach and play out an often-dreamed fantasy. Find your secluded bay, strip off your clothes, swim out as far as possible, then come back to shore. You are Robinson Crusoe swimming to land as the only survivor of an unfortunate shipwreck. Stranded on a deserted island, you must hone your survival skills. Find a coconut and split it open. This is lunch in your new home. Having surveyed the beach, now it's time to explore a bit. With a little luck, maybe you'll find Friday.

Outfitters & Resources

Nautilus Dive Center
382 Kamehameha Ave.
Hilo, HI 96720
☎ 808-935-6939
One of the only dive shops on the Hilo side. Ask for a free map to the best dive sites.

Paniolo Riding Adventures
PO Box 363
Honokaa, HI 96727
☎ 808-889-5354
Open range riding on the 11,000-acre Ponoholo working cattle ranch in the Kohala Mountains.

Teo's Safaris
In Keaau, just south of Hilo
☎ 808-982-5221
Rents mountain bikes and leads several fun rainforest rides.

Waipio Naalapa Trail Rides
PO Box 992
Honokaa, HI 96727
☎ 808-775-0419
Horseback excursions through Waipio Valley. Offers rides from Kukuihaele. Great storytelling guides.

Waipio Valley Wagon Tour
☎ 808-775-9518

HILO HELICOPTER COMPANIES
Hilo Bay Air
☎ 808-969-1545
Io Aviation
☎ 808-935-3031
Kainoa Aviation
☎ 808-961-5591

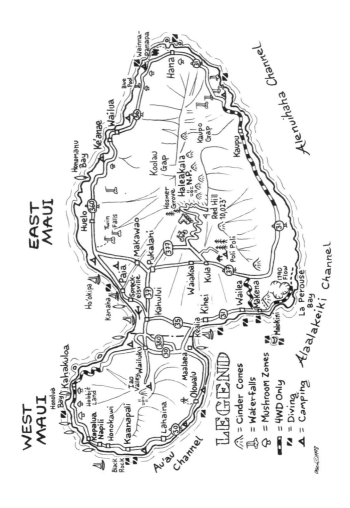

WEST MAUI

EAST MAUI

LEGEND

⛰ = Cinder Cones

💧 = Waterfalls

🍄 = Mushroom Zones

▄▄▄ = 4WD Only

⚓ = Diving

△ = Camping

MAUI

East Maui

"It was a scene of vast bleakness and desolation, stern, forbidding, fascinating... a workshop of nature cluttered with the raw beginnings of world-making." ~ Jack London, on first viewing Haleakala Crater

Everything in East Maui centers around, or is inside, the massive **Haleakala volcano c**one. Rising 10,023 feet into the tropical sky, from a sea-level base of 33 miles in diameter, Haleakala is the world's largest dormant volcano and holds many unusual distinctions. Working from the top down: **Haleakala National Park** contains an enormous crater at the top of the mountain – an immense bowl measuring 7.5 miles long, 2.5 miles wide, and .5 mile deep – which could easily accommodate the whole island of Manhattan. Along the upper slopes of Haleakala and inside the crater lives the rarest plant in the world, the **silversword**. The south-east slopes feature the globe's **greatest climatic change** in the shortest distance. Within one mile you can travel from a

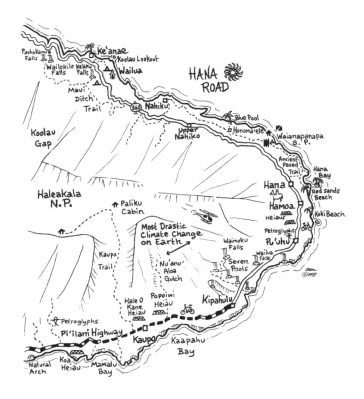

tropical rainforest on the windward side to desert conditions on the leeward side.

Archeological remains have been found inside the crater, yet there is no evidence the ancient Hawaiians ever made their homes in this hostile environment. Haleakala Crater was a very sacred place to the natives, and the literal translation of *Hale a ka la* means "House of the Sun." This is where the demigod Maui captured the sun and demanded that it take more time crossing the horizon every day. The sun complied, and Maui let it go. Although clouds usually shroud the lower slopes of Haleakala and sometimes fill the crater, the summit is often bathed in sunlight (thanks, again, to the god Maui). The impression everywhere is of dazzling light, and viewing the sunrise from the summit is as spectacular as it is popular.

In the realm of extreme adventures, East Maui comes shining through. A spot near the town of Paia (a hotel/resort haven) is considered the "**Windsurfing Capital of the World**" for its ideal, year-round conditions. From Paia, travel along the legendary **Hana Highway,** replete with 617 curves and many side excursions. The other large concentration of hotels and resorts is on the **Kihei-Wailea Coast**, famous for its splendid beaches, and noted for its excellent windsurfing and scuba diving. Don't worry about finding wilderness: East Maui is filled with radical hiking and waterfall excursions.

HALEAKALA CRATER EXCURSIONS

Haleakala National Park encompasses the upper slopes of the volcano, the crater itself, and the Kipahulu Valley down to the Oheo Gulch coastline (Seven Sacred Pools). Much of the rainforest and upper slopes are designated wilderness reserves and off-limits to people, ensuring that the primeval character of the area will remain. But not to worry, the 36 miles of trails in the Haleakala Crater wilderness cover a land of sudden contrasts and awesome terrain, not to mention varied topography. Weather changes rapidly in the crater. It is not uncommon to be exposed to intense sunlight one moment, then engulfed in thick clouds and heavy rains another. Altitude sickness and freezing temperatures at night also affect hikers. As the Boy Scouts would say, "Be Prepared!"

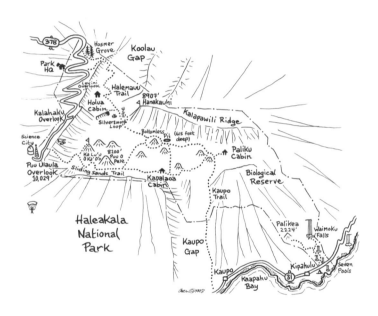

When everything is in order, you are about to embark on one of the most memorable hikes of your life. Where else can you amble among the world's rarest plants (the silversword), climb through lava tubes, and feel as though you're walking on the moon? It was Haleakala Crater, in fact, where NASA first test drove the lunar rovers in preparation for the Apollo moon missions. No space suits necessary and the gravity seems awfully close to earth. But hey, with a little imagination...

Sliding Sands Trail, Haleakala Crater

SINGLE-DAY CRATER TREK

 RISK: 2   **ADRENALINE: 6**

Perhaps the best single in-and-out day hike in Hawaii is right here. Start at the summit for a dazzling sunrise, then begin your hike down the **Sliding Sands Trail** to the crater floor. This vigorous 12-mile hike spans over 2,800 feet of elevation and covers some of the best terrain in the crater. Side excursions include a journey into **Ka Lu'u o ka 'O'o** cinder cone, the **bottomless pit** (615 feet deep), the **silversword loop**, and a **lava tube** near Holua Cabin. Mind you, side-trips cover more miles and will add time to your journey. Your objective is to make it up the final 3.9 miles of switchbacks on the **Halemauu Trail** before it gets dark, ascending 1,050 feet to the park road and trail's end where you – hopefully – left your car.

> ### TIP
>
> If you have only one car and need to catch a ride one way, it's much easier to hitchhike to the summit in the morning when there's heavy sunrise traffic. Two cars offer the best solution; leave one at the summit, the other at trail's end.

 ## FOUR-DAY CRATER TREK
RISK: 3   ADRENALINE: 8

A trek into Haleakala Crater is an extreme adventure to remember for a lifetime, so why rush it? With a little advance planning, you can secure your group the luxury of staying in the crater's three different cabins on consecutive nights. (See page 101 for contact.) All cabins are equipped with bunk beds (bring your own sleeping bag and foodstuff), basic kitchen utilities and a wood-burning stove. Otherwise, pitch a tent at Paliku or Holua campgrounds. Multi-day trips allow you the opportunity to take all the fascinating side-trips, and give you more time to marvel at Haleakala's desolate beauty. Submit your cabin or camping itinerary to make a big loop through the crater: Kapalaoa Cabin the first night; Paliku Cabin the second night; Holua Cabin the third night; and out of the crater on the fourth day.

KAUPO GAP TREK

RISK: 5   ADRENALINE: 8

This is the Granddaddy of all Hawaiian day treks. Hikers in excellent physical condition can take this 17.6-mile trek from the highest point on Maui, completely through the crater, and down the Kaupo Gap to sea level. It's a 9.8-mile hike to Paliku Cabin and 7.8 miles to Kaupo Village. Sturdy, well-fitting hiking boots are essential, as is a good supply of food and water. You will need someone to drop you off at the summit at sunrise, then meet you in Kaupo Village at the end of the day. Most hikers prefer to do the Kaupo Gap in one day so they don't have to carry a lot of camping supplies. Otherwise, try to get a reservation for Paliku Cabin to break up the trip.

BICYCLE EXCURSIONS

Mountain bikers have the distinct advantage of going where rental cars can't. A whole new arena of possibilities is opened up – from dirt roads in upcountry to King's Trail in La Perouse, past Makena. Feel free to tear down the beach access roads and never worry about parking.

```
WARNING...
Stay alert to the possibility
of theft. A strong bike lock
is as essential as your tube
repair kit and pump.
```

HALEAKALA DOWNHILL
RISK: 2   ADRENALINE: 6

One of the most popular outfitter excursions on Maui is the famous Haleakala Downhill.

Preparing for the ride down from Haleakala Crater.

You get picked up at your hotel when it's still dark out and make it to the summit of Haleakala for sunrise. After a dazzling sky-show from Mother Nature, pop on your helmet and saddle up! It's time to start a beautiful 38-mile downhill cruise from crater rim to sea level. Experienced cyclists may get frustrated waiting for slow "brake-riders," but with so much natural splendor to gaze upon, maybe frequent stops are just what you need to take it all in.

HANA TO ULUPALAKUA
RISK: 3   ADRENALINE: 4

While the Hana Highway would make a great bike ride, there are far too many ignorant tourists on this narrow road to make it safe for bicyclists. A better bet is to transport your bikes to Hana and ride from there. This remote route offers all the natural splendor of the Hana Road with much less traffic. Mountain bikers prepared for a multi-day excursion can carry on to the leeward coast along the Pi'ilani Highway, then drop down the dirt track to Makena Beach.

HANA HIGHWAY EXCURSIONS

The twisting and turning road to Hana is quite an experience. This 44-mile drive begins at Paia and passes by magnificent waterfalls, secluded swimming holes, remote beaches, lush tropical forests, and crosses over 50 one-lane bridges. Take your time on this road; not only is it one of the most beautiful drives in Hawaii, but it is the main artery to a full day of extreme adventures. Finish the day at Oheo Gulch (meaning Seven Sacred Pools), where you can pitch a tent and crash before the next day's excursions.

TWIN FALLS

RISK: 3   ADRENALINE: 3

The first stop is Twin Falls, 11 miles east of
Paia and just past the intersection of 365
from Makawao. Pull over at Mile Marker 2,
just before the bridge. Follow the obvious
footpath up the jeep trail until you hear the
sound of running water. This is the first of
the Twin Falls where, last we checked, there
was a great rope swing. A little farther up is
the second fall, which is equally beautiful
and perfect for a swim.

*Taking the
plunge at
Twin Falls.*

KEANAE PENINSULA EXCURSIONS

RISK: 3   **ADRENALINE: 4**

Around 24 miles past Paia is a turnout on the right side of the highway at Mile Marker 16 for the Keanae Arboretum. Park here to access a bunch of fun little side-trips. The **Arboretum Trail** is interesting, full of swimming holes and waterfalls. It's a two-hour hike, three miles round-trip. Continue farther and you will loop back to Wailokilo Falls, then to Puohokamoa Falls just off the highway at Mile Marker 11. Hitch five miles back to where you left the car. A quarter-mile down the highway is the turnoff for Keanae Village on the beautiful Keanae Peninsula.

WAIANAPANAPA STATE PARK

Three miles before you reach Hana on the Hana Highway is a simple "State Park" sign for the turnoff to the unbelievably cool Waianapanapa State Park. This park alone can easily provide a full day of radical excursions. There is a cabin your group can rent here, or else you can camp for free. As at Hana, there is a red and black sand beach for your lounging and exploring pleasures. Coastal hiking trails in either direction get you as far away from the crowds as you desire.

UNDERWATER CAVE

RISK: 9   *ADRENALINE: 6*

This adventure is strictly for strong swimmers who know what they're doing. A very short trail from the parking lot leads to the partially submerged lava tube called **Waianapanapa Cave**. At the entrance, put on your snorkel gear, get in the water and turn on your underwater flashlight. It's time to explore! Located at intervals of 6-12 feet is a series of air chambers where you can catch your breath. It is absolutely impossible to swim these caves if you are at all claustrophobic. Don't even attempt it. It is pitch dark down there so it's a pretty good idea to bring a back-up light. At the end of the lava tube is a large dry cave where you can get out and explore on foot. Look up for daylight in "Witch's Chimney."

KING'S TRAIL TO HANA
RISK: 2   ADRENALINE: 3

From the caves, follow the trail down to the sea and east toward Hana. This is the **Ancient Paved Trail**, also known as the King's Trail, which leads four miles to Hana. The trail takes you past lava flows, blowholes, and crashing surf underfoot. The rugged trail gets kinda confusing near the end, but just keep pressing on and you will eventually reach Hana.

A black lava arch looks out over the sea at Waianapanapa State Park.

SEVEN SACRED POOLS

About seven miles south of Hana is a place popularly known as the Seven Sacred Pools. While there are far more than seven pools here and there is nothing at all sacred about them (according to Hawaiian legend), the name is kinda catchy. The proper name is Oheo Gulch, and this land is part of Haleakala National Park. Free camping is allowed near the well-marked parking lot. Another mile past Oheo Gulch is Kipahulu, one of Hawaii's most beautiful and pristine valleys. Here begins a one-lane gravel road only suited for 4WD vehicles and mountain bikes.

LOWER POOL EXTREMITIES

 RISK: 9   **ADRENALINE: 6**

Nearly all the tourists visiting Oheo Gulch head straight for the lower falls. While this is a swell place to jump some puny falls and plunge down a natural water slide, there are far more extreme excursions in store. The first is an underwater cave connecting the two lower pools. If you can swim the length of a regular swimming pool (about 47 feet) underwater, you can do this. If you have any doubts about your abilities, or feel that you might panic mid-way, do not attempt this.

Probe around the water plunge pool until you spot light coming through from the other side. Get a big breath, and GO FOR IT!

The other major adventure is jumping off the highway bridge. There is an 'X' marking the spot on the bridge where those who are daring drop 55 feet to the narrow but very deep pool below.

> TIP
>
> Concentrate on dropping straight into the gap. Keep your arms together so they don't slap the water upon impact.

From this point you will have to jump a few more falls to get to the lower pools.

WAIMOKU FALLS HIKE

RISK: 2 **ADRENALINE: 4**

This four-mile round-trip hike will take you to one of the most spectacular waterfalls in Maui. The trail starts across the road from the parking lot, which leads through a meadow and then into a forest. Along the trail are edible mango, guava, thimble berry and mountain apples. Chow down! A good time to take a break is at the 185-foot **Makahiku Falls**, about a quarter of the way up. When you cross the Palikea Stream you will pass through the first of three bamboo groves before reaching the impressive 580-foot Waimoku Falls. Swim across the large pool to the fern grotto underneath the falls for a true jungle experience. Follow the trail back down the way you came until you reach...

★

POOLS JUMP

RISK: 5 **ADRENALINE: 8**

About half-way along the trail to Waimoku Falls you will come to the point where the Pipiwai and the Palikea Streams converge. In

the midst of a bamboo forest, the streams cascade from two waterfalls into a single pool below. Once you jump into this pool, it's very difficult to climb back out. While you may climb the opposite wall and jump into the pool again, you are basically committed to finishing this adventure. None of the jumps from this point on are much higher than the first 18-footer you've already braved, and all the pools are quite deep. So now the only way to go is down, one waterfall jump after the other, until you reach a long, meandering stream through a steep volcanic canyon. Relax as you float along, marveling at the tropical forest canopy overhead. At the end of the stream is a dam. Get out here and link back up to the Waimoku Falls Trail.

PARAGLIDE MAUI

Paragliders are the lightest and slowest form of flying aircraft in the world – so light and compact, most complete paragliding rigs can be stuffed into any normal-sized backpack and carried along to just about any precarious perch. Setup takes a few minutes and launches can be made in winds as light as five mph, yet winds stronger than 15 mph will keep most paragliders grounded.

> ## WARNING...
>
> Because an understanding of airflow characteristics and landing techniques is critical (your life could depend on it), it is imperative that all new pilots enroll in a training course.

Basic certification can be completed after as few as 20 hours of training and study. After certification, complete used paraglider rigs may be purchased for a thousand dollars. Subsequent launches are then forever free.

PARAGLIDE FROM THE
REDWOODS TO THE SEA

RISK: 5 ADRENALINE: 8

Most paragliding in Maui is done from the slopes of Haleakala Volcano, at around the 6,400-foot mark. Here is the little-visited **Polipoli State Park**, home to California redwoods planted in the 1930's. Reaching Polipoli is an adventure into some of Maui's remote reaches. From Kahului, take the Haleakala Highway (Route 37) through Pukalani and past Waiakoa to Route 377. Turn left on 377 and follow the signs to the park. The roads are sometimes muddy and four-wheel-drive is recommended.

Excellent hiking trails and launch pads found here are an extreme adventurer's dream. Hang gliders circle in the wind drafts and land nearby when they're finished. Paragliders, including tandems, take that one-way ticket down. One distinct advantage to paragliding from Polipoli is the number of alternative landing spots available. Popular landings are at Big and Little Makena beaches in front of hundreds of gawking tourists, but most likely your landing will be in one of the many flat and open cow pastures (sorry!).

DiViNG tHE WAiLEA COAST

Most of the good diving on East Maui is found along the Wailea Coast. This area is blocked from the rain by Haleakala and the seas are mostly calm. The earlier in the morning, the better the conditions. Snorkelers can choose just about any bay from Kihei to Makena and have a pretty good dive. Indeed, Makena is the focal point of most scuba divers' itineraries after they conquer nearby Molokini (see *Forbidden Islands*, page 228). Here are two classic Makena dives.

FIVE CAVES DIVE

RISK: 3   *ADRENALINE: 4*

This site is also called Five Graves or The Cemetery after the small cemetery on the coast which marks the entry point for a shore dive. (Look for the dirt road at Nahuna Point, just past the Makena Surf Condos on Makena Road.) This is also a popular boat dive for trips returning from Molokini. On the north side of the reef, running perpendicular to the shore, is a series of more than five caves. The caves are not very deep, only 40 feet, but extend quite a ways into the lava shelf. Turtles live around the caves and deep inside them reside several white-tip reef sharks. Although the sharks don't bother humans, it is still quite daunting to come face to face with one in a narrow cave. For this reason, and because of strong currents, only intermediate and advanced divers should come here.

 ## T ANK & L ANDING CRAFT
RISK: 4 ADRENALINE: 4

 In 60 feet of water off the coast of Makena is a WWII tank and landing craft. It is impossible to enter either one, but they're interesting to look at and swim around. The only way to find these coral-encrusted relics is to take a boat dive and have an instructor show you their location. This site is for intermediate or advanced divers only, as the currents can be rather strong.

WORLD'S WINDSURFING CAPITAL

Ever since a 13-year-old named Robbie Naish of Kailua won the first windsurfing championship in the 1970's, Hawaii has been regarded as a world-class sailboard destination. Hawaii is considered the spiritual home of the sport and many people in Maui devote their lives to windsurfing. "Hey man, it's what

I DO." If you want to windsurf where the die-hards do, don't stop where you see a lot of shiny new rental cars. You want to locate the salt-caked rustbuckets with surfing stickers keeping them intact.

World-class windsurfing all year round. That's what the coastline from Kahului past Paia has to offer. Every year, windsurfing events dominate the calendar. Here are a few of the biggies: Cemiesee Championship (early March); Maui O'Neill Pro Board (early April); Da Kine Classic (late May); Neil Pryde Slalom (early June); Hoyle Schweitzer Course Race (late June); Quicksilver Cup (early July); Hawaii State Championships (early August); and the Peter Stuyvesant Travel Aloha Classic (early November).

NOTE

Some of these venues and dates may change because of wind and wave conditions. For updates, call Maui Windsurfing, ☎ 800-972-0999, or contact the local Maui Marine Forecast, ☎ 808-877-3477.

KEALIA BEACH

 RISK: 3   ADRENALINE: 5

Somewhat shielded from the blasting winds on the high-profile beaches near Paia, Kealia Beach in Kihei is the place to come and learn windsurfing. No snobs here to look down on you, just a big wide-open bay to practice your jibes and waterstarts. Conditions are near ideal when it's windy, but not always as consistent as on the Paia side.

KANAHA BEACH

 RISK: 4   ADRENALINE: 5

With consistent easterly winds almost every day of the year, the Paia region of Maui attracts windsurfing fanatics from around the world. There is a whole industry on this side of the island catering to them. Rentals, lessons, equipment, accessories, surf safaris, even restaurants and budget motels suited for the sailboard clientele. Kanaha Beach is a good intermediate beach without the big jumping waves. But don't think Kanaha is kids' stuff – several major competitions are held here annually.

*Kahana
Beach*

HO'OKIPA BEACH

RISK: 9   **ADRENALINE: 8**

This is considered by the pros as not only the best windsurfing site on Maui, but the best windsurfing site in the *world*. Ho'okipa Beach has got everything: consistently strong winds over 300 days a year, and a submerged rocky ledge that produces huge 15-foot rolling waves. The aerial acrobats jump the waves with such speed and force that they compete for best air time maneuvers – and recovery landings. Needless to say, this is not a place for anyone except the pros. Ho'okipa Beach is located just below the highway two miles east of Paia.

Outfitters & Resources

Adventures on Horseback
PO Box 1771
Makawao, Maui, HI 96768
☎ 808-242-7445
Offers amazing horseback excursions to hidden waterfalls along the north coast.

Charley's Trail Rides & Pack Trips
c/o Charles Aki, Jr., Kaupo Store
Kaupo, Maui, HI 96713
☎ 808-248-8209
Daily guided trail rides and mule packtrips. Overnights or day-trips offered.

Crater Bound
PO Box 265
Kula, Maui, HI 96790
☎ 808-878-1743
Mule rides, Haleakala camping & van tours.

Cruiser Bob's
99 Hana Hwy., Box B
Paia, Maui, HI 96779
☎ 808-579-8444 or 800-654-7717
Offers the classic 40-mile bike cruise from the top of Haleakala down to the sea. Two meals, helmet, and bike use included. Cruiser Bob's also offers bicycle rentals.

Dive and Sea Center
1975 S. Kihei Road
Kihei, Maui, HI 96753
☎ 808-874-1952
*Full-service dive shop offering certification
courses, excursions and equipment rentals.*

Haleakala National Park
PO Box 369
Makawao, Maui, HI 96768
☎ 808-572-9306 (8am - 3pm)
*Cabin reservations must be submitted at
least two months in advance. Calls
regarding cabin vacancies are accepted only
from 1 to 3pm daily; a major credit card is
needed to secure reservations by phone.*

Hang Gliding Maui
☎ 808-572-6557

Maui Dive Shop
Azeka II Shopping Center, S. Kihei Road
Kihei, Maui, HI 96753
☎ 808-879-3388
*Offers scuba gear rental, instruction and
retail shop. Also runs excursions to Molokini
and other locations.*

Maui Downhill
199 Dairy Rd.
Kahului, Maui, HI 96732
☎ 808-871-2155 or 800-535-BIKE
*Offers the classic 40-mile bike cruise from
the top of Haleakala down to the sea. Two
meals, helmet, and bike use included.*

Prodiver Maui, Inc.
PO Box 828
Kihei, Maui, HI 96753
☎ 808-875-4004
Offers scuba gear rental, instruction and retail shop. Excursions to Molokini and other locations.

Proflyght Paragliding
☎ 808-874-5433

Sailboards Maui
430 Alamaha, Suite #103
Kahului, Maui, HI 96732
☎ 808-871-7954
Windsurfing rental and instructions.

South Pacific Kayaks
2439 S. Kihei Road
Kihei, Maui, HI 96753
☎ 808-875-4848 or 800-776-2326
Kayak instruction, rentals and excursions. Tours include lunch and snorkeling.

West Maui

> *"I still remember, with a sense of indolent luxury, a picnicking excursion up a romantic gorge there, called the Iao Valley. The trail lay along the edge of a brawling stream in the bottom of the gorge – a shady route, for it was well roofed with the verdant domes of forest trees. Through openings in the foliage we glimpsed picturesque scenery that revealed ceaseless changes and new charms with every step of our progress."* ~
> Mark Twain, *Roughing It*

Early Polynesian settlers arrived on Maui around AD 350 and lived mostly along the coast. The ancient land sections, or *ahupuaa*, divided West Maui like spokes of a wheel from the summit downwards. Thus, each tribe had its own seashore for fishing, flat lands for growing, uplands for gathering, as well as access to the higher portions for worship. The West Maui Mountains, especially the Iao Valley, were considered sacred lands to the Hawaiian people. Several *heiaus* can be found at high and remote locations, as can petroglyphs depicting tribal life.

West Maui is home to the historical and lively town of **Lahaina**. King Kamehameha the Great ruled his empire from Lahaina, and not long after his death it became a bustling whaling town. Lahaina was a seaside Sodom in the eyes of the newly arriving missionaries, who attacked the whalers for their wild living and countless sins. Tensions ran high, and one infamous moment saw the sailors rioting in the streets and firing their cannon at the mission homes for outlawing prostitution. It wasn't until the whaling industry bottomed out in the 1870's that the missionaries could really establish themselves. And establish themselves they did. There is a Hawaiian saying that sums up the 19th century well: "The missionaries came to do good, and they did very well."

Actually, it was the sone of the missionary preachers who did very well – usurping native land at an alarming pace. By the end of the century, white plantation owners would possess four times as much land as all the Hawaiian commoners combined. But back in Lahaina, the missionary fathers cleaned up the town, dressed the natives, and established a schooling system that would make Maui one of the most literate places on earth. Indeed, Lahaina was home to the first printing press west of the Rocky Mountains.

Contemporary Lahaina is a good place to start your explorations of Maui. It is also a good place to find housing and look for a job in nearby Kaanapali if you wish to reside on "The Valley Isle" for any length of time. For those seeking extreme fun and adventures, it is also a good base for action. Rooms in Lahaina's **Pioneer Inn** (650 Wharf Street; ☎ 661-3636) are very reasonable, the nightlife is happening, and most of the best adventures are a day-trip from town. After some time in Maui you will come to understand its ancient motto: *"Maui no ka oi"* (Maui is the best).

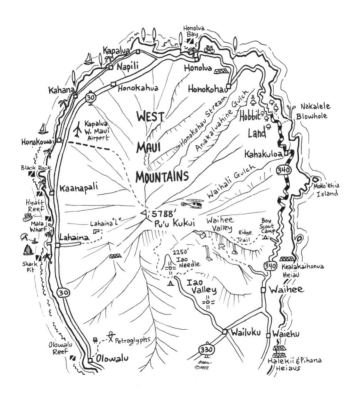

iAO VALLEY

Three miles up the road from the sleepy town of Wailuku, begins the most impressive and sacred valley on the island. Long a place of pilgrimage for ancient Hawaiians, Iao Valley became notorious as the site of Kamehameha's 1790 victory over the defenders of Maui. This battle was so horrible, the corpses blocking Kepaniwai Stream lent the name "damming of the waters," and Wailuku literally means "bloody river." Today it could be called "tourist river," after the countless thousands who arrive in tour buses to ascend the river valley every day for their quick peek.

IAO VALLEY HIKE

 RISK: 3 ADRENALINE: 4

Unfortunately, nobody can climb the impressive Iao Needle. Rising 1,200 feet from the valley floor, this moss-clad lava pinnacle is sacred, as well as pretty vertical. Leave it be. Hikes in the valley include various stream stomps to random swimming holes, and a trail leading up to an overlook of the Needle. Near the top of the stairs that lead to the overlook, you can pick up an overgrown trail and hike for two more miles on your way to rarely visited places. It is advisable to come in the morning before clouds and rain move into the valley. Then you can find your own secluded pool and go skinny dipping.

OTHER WEST MAUI HKES

OLOWALU PETROGLYPHS
RISK: 1   ADRENALINE: 1

Nothing drastic here, but interesting just the same. When you're in the Olowalu area, stop by the General Store for a drink and check out some ancient Hawaiian petroglyphs. Follow the trail behind the store until you come to a water tank on the left. Stay on the sugarcane road until you reach a volcanic outcropping. The images are on the face of a hillside and depict humans and animals in a tribal setting. A good place to bring drums and digeredoos. The trip covers about a mile.

WAIHEE VALLEY
RISK: 4   ADRENALINE: 6

Indiana Jones would like one. Starting in the beautiful Waihee Valley (turn inland onto Waihee Valley Road, 10 miles south of Kahakuloa); the trail starts in dense fern pasture and gets more radical with every step. Soon you will be in a lush rainforest with waterfalls cascading down steep cliff walls. Old banyan trees add to the effect, but the best are two rope bridges you must cross. There is also a time you must ford the river.

> **WARNING...**
>
> If the river is running swift, or if it is raining, turn back. These rivers fill up quickly and can sweep hikers off their feet.

If you can make it, the reward is a dam with an excellent swimming hole near its base. Four miles round-trip.

PU'U KUKUI WEST MAUI SUMMIT

RISK: 9   *ADRENALINE: 7*

The most difficult hike on Maui is to the upper reaches of 5,788-foot Pu'u Kukui Mountain. The trail begins at the end of a sugarcane road that extends from the town of Honokawai. Experienced hikers will have to do some bushwhacking, but the round-trip is possible within a day. Like the Alakai Swamp in Kauai (see page 200), hikers will cross a bizarre high-altitude swamp. It rains here a lot. The summit is too wet for camping, but there is an old shelter up there where you can rest. Start early and be prepared for harsh elements, namely rain, mud, and cold.

MOUNTAIN BIKING WEST MAUI

The ride from Lahaina to Kapalua is pretty sedate, going past one resort community after another. When Highway 30 changes to Highway 340 at Honokohau Bay, then the fun begins. Here the paved road becomes a rutted dirt track, which tourists in rental cars are not allowed to drive. Traffic becomes thin and the scenery ever more spectacular. Actually, the road you're following was an old royal Hawaiian foot trail, which takes you to the more sacred side of West Maui. In the **Kahakuloa Valley** you'll pass around hairpin turns, steep cliffs and lush fern gulches. Every new turn is a treat for the eyes. Just look at the razorback ridges running down from Pu'u Kukui's mile-high summit to the crashing sea below. After the road becomes paved again in the sugarcane town of Waihee, take a side-trip to one of the many enormous *heiaus* on this part of the island.

Victorious after a West Maui bike ride.

MOUNTAIN BIKE CAMPING AROUND WEST MAUI

RISK: 3 ADRENALINE: 5

The best way to do this ride is with some camping gear. Stretch it out for a couple of days. It covers some of the most scenic and secluded regions in Maui and shouldn't be rushed. Spend one or two days exploring the deserted valleys and beaches, especially along the Kahekili Highway section between Kahakuloa and Waihee. Pitch a tent on the beach, (Honolua Bay first night, Hobbit Land second night) or in the cane fields and macadamia nut groves farther along the road. Nobody should hassle you.

Kahakuloa, on the way to Hobbit Land.

HOBBIT LAND

One of the finest places to stop and wander is an area known as Hobbit Land. You will know you are there when you see a surrealistic field covered with hundreds of cairns, which are man-made stacks of rocks. Build your own hobbit tower (cairn) for good luck. Hike down past the lighthouse to some lava-flow formations. There is a trail leading to **Nakalele Blowhole** near the rough and crashing surf.

MAGIC MUSHROOM HUNT
RISK: 5   PSYCHEDELIC: 5

The meadows of Hobbit Land are private cow pastures, and the bovines make sure the grass is grazed to golf course levels. After a rainfall – quite frequent on the windward side – spores from psychedelic mushrooms attach themselves to cow dung and grow like crazy. A popular pastime with the hippie-stoner crowd is to come to Hobbit Land after or during a rain and pick some magic mushys. People who know what they look like (no description here – go with someone who knows!) pop 'em as they find 'em and blaze away in Maui's most psychedelic misty-trippy landscape!

SURFING ETIQUETTE

First of all, surfing on Maui is very popular among local young men. There is a whole sub-culture associated around the sleek, waxed-up surfboard. During the fall and winter surf season, the picture-perfect six-foot swell is sought by many. You, as a mainland *haole*, have little clout with the local boyz, no matter how good you surf. Thus, cutting in on ideal days can get you in on big trouble. This territory is considered theirs, *kapu* to you.

SURFING WITH THE NATIVES

Now hold it, are you telling me I can't surf Maui? Well, yes and no. Yes, go with your board and go out when the winter swells are pounding. No, do not go into the middle of a big crowd. Avoid them. Surf inshore, surf on less than ideal days, or go to the outer reef for those sporadic good breaks. Try and get to know a local, or become one, so you are at least tolerated. DO NOT go out there with an attitude. Sorry, these are not everybody's waves, and you will get yourself into a fight if you try and argue. Just be cool, and approach surfing in Maui as an incremental PROCESS. Then, and only then, can you surf the prime waves on prime days. *Shaka, brah!*

Catching A Wave

1. Position your body, face down,
   on the deck of your surfboard.
2. Check the perimeter of your surfboard
   for sharks (or worse, angry locals).
3. Insert cupped hands into water and
   swing arms in a circular motion.
4. When surf begins to undulate, maneuver
   your board in front of oncoming wave.
5. As vehicle begins to propel forward,
   clutch both sides of board to establish a center of gravity. Using arms,
   quickly lift body off of surfboard.
6. Position both feet on deck of board
   and try to stand erect.
7. Prepare to be thrashed immediately.
8. Once you have retrieved your board,
   repeat steps 1-7 until you
   decide to call it a day.

SURFING WEST MAUI

The great thing about surfing West Maui is that there is something for everybody. Beginners, and even intermediate surfers, don't have to fear angry locals. The big swells are what they prize, and only advanced surfers should heed the aforementioned warning. During the winter storm season, small, medium and large waves can be found in a multitude of north shore locations on Maui. Ask around and try to pick an area that is right for you. On the north shore you have Honokohau Bay, Honolua Bay, Mokuleia Bay (Slaughterhouse), Honokahua Bay and Napili Bay. You can surf moderate-sized harbor breaks in Lahaina and Ma'alaea, where there are good breaks south of the harbor. Hard-core surfers with a fax machine can get the latest conditions from **Hawaii Faxcast**, 808-337-9509.

 ### HONOLUA BAY

RISK: 7 ADRENALINE: 6

After a winter storm, when the northern waves come rolling to land, Honolua Bay becomes a world-class surfing location. Here is the home of the Rusty Pro Surf Meet every year at the beginning of February. (Unfortunately, this is a locals-only event, but worth taking in as a spectator all the same.) Under the water, Honolua Bay is a Marine Life Conservation District, perfect for summer snorkeling and scuba diving. In the winter it's a prime surf location. Some of the waves can get as high as 20 feet, not as big as the north shore of Oahu, but pretty challenging nonetheless!

SCUBA DiVING LOCATIONS

West Maui is almost like another island altogether. The mountains are different, the valleys are different, the contour of the coastline is different, and thus, the diving is different. Since the West Maui Mountains catch so much rain (this is the second wettest spot in the world), the leeward coast is dry and calm all year round. Even during the most extreme winter swells, the protected enclaves of West Maui are still safe for diving – probably another reason why tourism has exploded here in the last few decades.

HONOLUA BAY

RISK: 3   ADRENALINE: 4

Honolua Bay is a beautiful secluded marine sanctuary. The fish are tame, the coral interesting, and the visibility excellent. The coral starts in only five feet of water, so this is an equally great spot for snorkeling and scuba diving. Although you have to carry your gear about a quarter-mile from the parking lot, the rock and sandy beach allows for unproblematic entry. Actually, beach dives are extremely easy, and for this reason night diving here has become quite popular. Near the entrance to the bay are several archways and a 40-foot wall. Most of the crabs are found in the wall, and larger marine animals come up from the depths near here. After the spring and summer diving season comes to an end, in the fall and winter Honolua Bay becomes a premiere surfing location.

OLOWALU DIVE

RISK: 2   **ADRENALINE:** 2

Site of the infamous 1790 massacre where an American merchant ship opened fire on hundreds of innocent natives, Olowalu today is a sleepy little town. Most come here for the long sandy beach and excellent snorkeling. In fact, more people come here to snorkel than to scuba dive. The trouble with shore diving is that you have to pass a long, shallow reef before you can drop down. Thus, most opt to take a boat out here for diving. Once in the depths, the colorful reef is home to huge amounts of tropical fish and green sea turtles. The terrain is pretty much the same for many miles and currents are generally very light. Great spot for novice divers.

KAANAPALI HOTEL REEF

RISK: 2   **ADRENALINE:** 3

A long reef lies off the coast of Kaanapali, extending from Black Rock all the way past the big hotels. The most notable spot for diving is offshore from the Hyatt Regency

Resort, now known as Hyatt Reef. Coral clusters, large varieties of tropical fish, and sea turtles inhabit the area. Most divers choose to take a boat out here in order to avoid the sometimes dangerous beach approach. The outer edge of the reef lies in 40-60 feet of water and houses a nice ledge where the turtles hang out. When the reef picks up a second time near Lahaina, it again offers some fine snorkeling spots. Most memorable are **Mala Wharf** north of town, and **Shark Pit**, just south of town.

BLACK ROCK

Black Rock is a huge lava formation located at the Sheraton Hotel on Kaanapali Beach. This site is popular with snorkelers and scuba divers alike for its easy shore access and interesting lava formations. In the 20-30 feet depths you will also discover abundant marine life and great visibility. The protective cove is a learning center for new divers and very popular as a night dive. Scuba divers can venture farther out on the lava peninsula for more holes and creatures. But Black Rock is equally exciting *without* tanks on your back.

BLACK ROCK CLIFF
JUMP & SNORKEL

RISK: 5   ADRENALINE: 3

On the north side of Black Rock is a sheer 40-foot cliff. Swim the depths first to locate the water landing. Once you know the spot, climb back up, and throw your snorkel gear off the cliff. Walk back 20 feet on the grass. On the count of three, everybody goes running for the edge. It's quite a spectacle as you and your friends are all flying through the air down to the blue sea below. Once in the water, swim down 20 feet and retrieve your gear, then snorkel around the point back to Kaanapali.

PARTY DOWN IN LAHAINA TOWN

As Maui's top tourist destination, Lahaina attracts untold thousands with its ramshackle storefronts and old charm image. This historic town was a seat for royal Hawaiians since the 16th century, a major whaling port in the early 1800's, and home to the first printing press east of the Rockies in 1831. Today it is a full-service, full-blown tourist town, replete with glittery art galleries, falsefront stores, and hawking activity salesmen (a job this author did for a year or so).

Like their boisterous whaler forbears, locals and tourists alike need to blow off a little steam. No longer will you find uninhibited naked women swimming out to meet your ship, but you will find enough bars and taverns to keep you happy until late at night. Like a drunken sailor, you'll be pleased to know that most watering holes lie within a half-mile of the old sea wall that props up Front Street. The best way to explore Lahaina is on foot.

PUB CRAWL

RISK: 4   **DRUNKENESS: 6**

To fully capture the spirit of old Lahaina Town, there's only one place to start (and/or finish) your pub crawl: the banyan tree in front of the **Pioneer Inn** (650 Wharf Street; ☎ 661-3636). The 120-year-old tree and the rickety old hotel/saloon are right on the waterfront and smack dab in the middle of town. The inn is noisy, vibrant, and crowded, and no one here sleeps until the saloon closes at 1 a.m. In the Pioneer Inn's rustic **Old Whaler's Grog Shop**, choose the standard fare and have the barkeep pour you a glass of rum. If this saloon doesn't conjure up images of life during the rowdy days when Lahaina was the whaling capital of the world, you obviously don't have a lively imagination. This place has a very old-time nautical thing going, complete with harpoons, figureheads, and paintings of naked ladies. Live music is usually country, blues or jazz. By the way, the Pioneer Inn is the best value hotel in Maui – if you can stand the noise.

Now you're out on Front Street, the party capital of Maui. Options abound. If Maui is experiencing yet another mind-blowing sunset, you'll want to make your way to a few of the terrace restaurant/bars famous for sunset decadence. Tops on the list are **Kimo's** (845 Front Street; ☎ 661-4811), **Lahaina Broiler** (885 Front Street; ☎ 661-3111), and the ultra-flashy **Longhi's** (888 Front Street; ☎ 667-2288). After 10 p.m., a hopping club is **Moose McGillycuddy's** (☎ 667-7758) on Front Street. The Moose drinks are inventive and strong, the dancefloor loose and wild. Out of town on the Honoapiilani Highway back to Kaanapali, stop by **Blackie's Bar** (☎ 667-7979) for live jazz four days a week.

Those low on cash report having a great time hanging out on the seawall with a 40 Ounce, just watching all the activity. People-watching can be the best part of a night out here, especially on the last day in October when thousands descend into Lahaina to celebrate Halloween. This is one of the wildest costume parties in the world. The **Halloween Mardi Gras of the Pacific** should not to be missed.

Outfitters & Resources

Fantasy Island Activities and Tours
☎ 808-698-2001
Booking agency in Lahaina that can set you up on any trip for Maui, Lanai, and Molokai.

Fun Rentals of Maui
193 Lahainaluna Road
Lahaina, Maui, HI 96761
☎ 808-661-3053
Rents skim boards, surfboards and boogie boards at reasonable daily and weekly rates.

Hawaiian Reef Divers
156 Lahainaluna Road
Lahaina, Maui, HI 96761
☎ 808-667-7647
Offers scuba gear rental, instruction and excursions.

Lahaina Divers
710 Front Street
Lahaina, Maui, HI 96761
☎ 808-667-7496
Offers scuba gear rental, instruction, excursions and retail shop.

Mango Mitch Ecotours
PO Box 2511
Wailuku, Maui, HI 96793
☎ 808-875-9106
Single- and multiple-day eco-camping and hiking tours around the island.

Maui Windsurfing Company
520 Keolani Place
Kahului, Maui, HI 96732
☎ 808-877-4816 or 800-872-0999
Windsurfing rental, instruction and retail shop.

Nancy C. Emerson School of Surfing
PO Box 463
Lahaina, Maui, HI 96767
☎ 808-874-2581 http://maui.net/~ncesurf/ncesurf.html
Surf pro turned instructor claims anyone can learn to surf in one lesson.

Rainbow Ranch
PO Box 10066
Lahaina, Maui, HI 96761
☎ 808-669-4991
Full-day and half-day horseback excursions in the West Maui Mountains.

HELICOPTER COMPANIES
Alex Air
☎ 808-871-0792
Blue Hawaiian
☎ 808-871-8844
Hawaii Helicopter

☎ 800-346-2403
Kenai Helicopter
☎ 800-622-3144
Papillon
☎ 800-562-5641
Sunshine
☎ 800-544-2520

PARASAIL COMPANIES
Lahaina Parasail
☎ 808-661-4887
Para-Sail Hawaii
☎ 808-661-5322
UFO Parasail
☎ 808-661-7UFO
West Maui Parasail
☎ 808-661-4060

LANAI

Ua Mau Ke Ea O Ka Aina I Ka Pono "*The life of the land is perpetuated in righteousness.*" ~ Hawaii State Motto

Long regarded as the "Pineapple Island" because of favorable growing conditions, pineapple production ceased on the island in the early 1990's due to increased labor costs. A better name today would be the "Private Island"; 98% of the land of Lanai is owned by one person – David H. Murdock of Castle & Cooke corporation. Needless to say, the transition from an agricultural economy to one based on exclusive tourism has been a rough ride for some of the locals. Resentment runs high for Mr. Murdock (no relation to the media mogul).

In simpler times, Lanai was not chosen as a home by Polynesians, who thought the island contained far too many evil spirits. The son of a Maui chief, a wild prince named Kaululaau, was exiled to Lanai, did away with the evil spirits and thus paved the way for settlement. While the native population never exceeded 2,500 (about the same as it is today), it had been the summer residence for King Kamehameha the Great and other warrior kings. The reason Lanai was favored is largely due to its vantage points – from here it is possible to see all the Hawaiian islands except Kauai and Niihau. This made it easy to monitor the seas for attack, or prepare to defend if a war party was en route. Its name is far more innocent. Lanai in Hawaiian means "hump," and the land truly does resemble a humpback whale about to submerge.

The island as a whole is pretty dry. Don't expect jungle and waterfalls here; Maui catches most of the rain. This makes the Lahaina Roads (Au'au Channel) nice and calm in the winter – perfect for watersports and whale-watching. The flat plateau and miles of dirt track offer ideal conditions for touring the island on a mountain bike. Hike or bike up the Munro Trail to 3,370-foot Lanaihale Peak. Venture farther and discover interesting petroglyphs and Hawaii's largest *heiau*. Or do nothing but wander along an abandoned beach – Lanai is full of them. Underwater enthusiasts regard the south shore of Lanai as having some of the best dive locations in Hawaii. The "Private Island" offers wilderness solitude rarely found, without being too far away from civilization.

MOUNTAIN BIKE ADVENTURES

The majority of visitors come to Lanai by boat, and the most popular way is aboard the *Expeditions* ferry from Lahaina, Maui to Manele Bay, five times daily. The adult fare is $25 each way, and riders may bring along their bicycles for $10 extra. From Manele it is a long, hot three-mile uphill ride to the 1,600-foot **Palawai Basin**. Once on top of the flat plateau, it's pretty easy riding to Lanai City and beyond.

> ### TIP
>
> Remember, the last ferry back to Maui is at 6:45 p.m. sharp! Otherwise, let's hope you brought along your camping gear.

Lanai is not a big island. As the sixth largest in the chain, it measures only 18 miles long and 13 miles wide. Thus, mountain bikers can access pretty much any part of the island within a day. But why rush it? With so few people and so much privacy, it is easy to do a multiple-day camping/riding excursion without any hassles. Multiple-day? Why not go for multiple weeks, where your only trouble will be riding up to Lanai City for more supplies.

MUNRO TRAIL RIDE
RISK: 2   ADRENALINE: 5

The Munro Trail begins about a mile out of Lanai City, off Keomuku Road. A pretty good ascent starts right away and can be rough going at times. But those who persist are rewarded with magnificent views from windswept heights. There are side trails out to Hookio and Hauola Gulch overlook, where you'll look over the deepest canyons on the island. The trail goes right up to the top of 3,370-foot **Mount Lanaihale**, which offers a panorama of every Hawaiian island except Kauai. Continue on down the southern track, which eventually becomes Hoike Road and ends at Route 440. Easily doable in a day.

GHOST TOWNS IN LANAI?

It's hard to believe that in the mega-expensive real estate market of Hawaii there could be such a thing as a ghost town. Well, on the eastern shores of Lanai there are a few. Most are totally overgrown and difficult to locate, but they are here. The majority are former sugar settlements that shut down in the early 20th century when the sweet water used to irrigate the sugar turned brackish. The locals told the bossman not to use the sacred stones from the *heiaus* to construct the foundation for the plantation, but he didn't listen. The whole operation went bust shortly thereafter.

KEOMUKU
GHOST TOWN RIDE

 RISK: 2   ADRENALINE: 5

A mile past Lanai City is the start of Keomuku Road, a long hairball ride down to the coast. Turn left to old Federation Camp and Shipwreck Beach, then make a right to Keomuku ghost town. Keomuku is most easily found by locating the old church, about six miles down the road. It's another mile and a half to *Kahea Heiau,* that troublesome site which spelled doom for the Maunalei Sugar Company. Not much farther on is Club Lanai, a fun little spot for Maui day-trippers. Near here is an old sugarcane locomotive lost in the thicket. A few miles farther up is the old Hawaiian village of Naha, where nothing but ghosts reside.

THE GARDEN OF THE GODS

Seven miles outside of Lanai City are the arid wastelands of northwestern Lanai known as the Garden of the Gods. Nothing much grows except shrubs among the exposed sand and rock. The varicolored canyon of windswept smoothness takes on an otherworldly appearance, especially the weird black rock formations you see everywhere. The bizarre material between the formations is an alchemist's blend of decomposed lava. The material takes on many different hues after being colored by sun, wind, and rain.

MOUNTAIN BIKING TO THE GARDEN OF THE GODS AND BEYOND!

 RISK: 2   **ADRENALINE:** 3

The Garden of the Gods is an unusual conglomeration of lava and multicolored boulders. The ride is pretty easy on paved and gravel tracks. Take the right fork at the only point where the route may seem uncertain. When the road starts sloping, you will gain a fantastic view of Molokai and this surreal red world. Continue on this road to Polihua Beach, a wide, white sandy stretch with good swimming and outstanding fishing. About a mile southwest from

Polihua Beach is the largest *heiau*. Time your ride to come back to the Garden of the Gods during sunset when the whole place seems to glow and the rock towers cast thousands of long, eerie shadows.

RAFTING AROUND THE ISLAND

If you're staying in Maui and don't have more than a day to see Lanai, sign up for an adventure raft trip around the island. It leaves early in the morning from Mala Wharf (roughly between Lahaina and Kaanapali); pure excitement lasts the entire day. For maximum bounce, secure a spot in the front of the raft. Call **Ocean Riders** at ☎ 808-661-3586 to make reservations.

ZODIAC RAFTING AROUND LANAI

 RISK: 2   ADRENALINE: 5

After crossing the Au'au Channel, the first stop is a morning snorkel along Lanai's diver-friendly south shore. From here it's not far to many of the island's most famous historical sites. Because the trip is made in a highly maneuverable Zodiac raft, calm days allow your driver to take you into narrow coves and even some fully enclosed sea caves! On the backside are mile after mile of fabulous 1,000-foot sea cliffs. Lunch is served on a private backside beach where the crew challenges riders to a game of touch football. The trip finishes on the north coast, where you will raft up close to several long-lost shipwrecks permanently parked on the nasty northern reef.

DiVinG LAnAi'S SOUTH COAST

Extending the full-length of Lanai's southern shore are an amazing conglomeration of coral reefs, lava formations, drop-offs, and underwater caves for the delight of snorkelers and scuba divers alike. The calm waters year-round pretty much guarantee successful outings every time, except during a rare southerly swell. For those who have never scuba dived before but have longed for the experience, this is the perfect opportunity to try an introductory dive. First-timers are instructed on the boat ride over from Maui, then closely supervised once underwater. This is the way to go if you don't have enough time to get certified!

FIRST & SECOND CATHEDRALS

RISK: 4

ADRENALINE: 6

What a deal – two incredible scuba dive playgrounds in the same trip. For an underwater cave experience like no other, book a dive trip to the Cathedrals on the southern shore of Lanai. First Cathedral features three 65-foot pinnacles extending upwards nearly to the water's surface. When viewed from below, they create a surreal "cathedral" appearance. The light reflecting down on all the colorful fish and coral lend the stained-glass and medieval look you would expect in one of Europe's finest. Piercing through the pinnacles are many tunnels and archways to explore, including an enormous grotto, home to hundreds of sea creatures.

Second Cathedral is not nearly as stunning as First, yet a great dive nonetheless. This dive is down a single hollow pinnacle. A flashlight is necessary once you enter the gigantic room, and it will allow you to see hidden creatures unlike those in the sunlit reefs. Unique coral, pink-eyed lobsters, and silvery ghost shrimp look pretty bizarre in this darkened underwater environment.

Both Cathedrals are considered intermediate dives and are accessible by boat only.

Between the two Cathedrals is **Hulopoe Bay**, a wonderful camping spot on a postcard-perfect palm-fringed beach. Snorkelers and scuba divers enjoy the clear waters and interesting coral in this virtually untouched underwater marine park. Hulopoe Bay is widely regarded as one of the top snorkeling spots in the entire island chain.

SERGEANT MAJOR & KNOB HILL

RISK: 2   *ADRENALINE: 3*

If the seas are surging when you get out to Lanai, the Divemaster may choose to avoid the potentially dangerous caves of the Cathedrals. In that case, you will probably dive Sergeant Major, a huge reef shelf populated with sergeant major fish. There is a long tunnel poking through one of the shelves, as well as a number of other caves to explore. Many tropicals and sea turtles live in the reefs here.

Another popular alternative to Cathedrals is Knob Hill, named after a huge lava rock which comes to within 15 feet of the surface.

Underneath the rock are several caves and non-dangerous white-tip sharks. Beyond the caves are two ridges extending into deeper water where you will likely spot a moray eel, scorpionfish and octopus. This site, like the Cathedrals, can surge during a southern swell.

LIGHTHOUSE REEF & SHARK FIN REEF

 RISK: 5   ADRENALINE: 5

Two amazing reefs on the southwestern tip of Lanai are the furthest from the shore and least visited. Lighthouse Reef is protected by a natural breakwater jutting from the lighthouse. It provides near-perfect calm conditions. Just be sure not to swim past the point where currents become strong. Where the dive boats anchor is a vertical wall leading to a picturesque archway. Beyond the arch, follow the wall to the right where two deep lava tubes begin. Bring a flashlight and avoid stirring-up silt on the bottom. Advanced divers only!

Just beyond the lighthouse is a tiny lava island which resembles the dorsal fin of a shark. Most divers drop-in on the northeast side of Shark Fin Reef and are immediately greeted by hungry fish hoping for a hand-out. Twenty feet below is an archway to swim through, also frequented by large jacks and rays. Follow the ridge around to the southern side where there is a submerged pinnacle and three caves.

WHALE-WATCHING IN AU'AU CHANNEL

Every year, humpback whales converge in the warm waters between Maui, Molokai, and Lanai to give birth. Since the gestation period of humpback is 11 months, this is also a winter mating ground (locals joke that it's the same for mainland honeymooners). The whales begin their migration at the end of an Alaskan feeding-frenzy summer and uniformly arrive at the Lahina Roads during November. The best whale-watching season is between January and April.

Humpbacks are quite playful animals and are commonly seen splashing, leaping and flapping their 15-foot tails over their backs. Humpbacks are unique in that they are the only whales with the ability to sing. Resonating with high and low pitches, their songs carry for many miles below the water. Sometimes, the noise can even be heard above the water. Researchers have recently discovered that humpback songs change entirely every year, yet, amazingly, all the whales seem to know the current version!

WHALE SWIM

RISK: 8   ADRENALINE: 9

Harassing any sea mammal in the Hawaiian Islands is strictly *kapu* (forbidden). There are stiff fines for anybody caught intentionally swimming out to see the whales or dolphins. These docile animals have put up with enough from humans; they deserve a break in Hawaii. Besides, many female humpbacks are having their babies just offshore. It's also a place they like to rest, especially near the outer reef between Federation Camp and Club Lanai, where there is hardly any human activity. You can't be fined, however, if the animals come swimming by you while you're diving. Something to keep in mind when scouting the reef you want to explore – there is nothing to compare with the sight of a humpback whale in the open sea.

SHIPWRECK BEACH ADVENTURES

Turn left at the bottom of Keomoku Road. This road will take you past a nearby ghost town called Federation Camp. It's actually a collection of shantytown colonies built from old shipwreck scraps in the 1950's by Filipino plantation workers. Today it's all but abandoned and mostly covered in vegetation, but some of the shacks are still used by the occasional squatter. At the end of the dirt road, look for a path marked with white paint. This trail will lead down into a gully full of big brown boulders and petroglyphs. This cluster depicts various scenes from everyday Hawaiian life.

 ## SHIPWRECK BEACH JOG
RISK: 4   ADRENALINE: 5

For those who love to beach jog, there is no better, more interesting stretch than Shipwreck Beach. It's a six-mile run from one big wreck to the other, another two to Polihua Beach. The entire distance is more like a series of sandy patches, sometimes over lava and coral, so running shoes are necessary. There is a smaller wreck closer to shore after the first mile. Along the way you will see many interesting objects, including glass fishing balls washed-up all the way from Japan!

LUAHIWA PETROGLYPHS

The Luahiwa petroglyphs are some of the best preserved and most detailed to be found on any island. Each boulder shows a different pictographic story of Hawaiian history. There are human figures, turtles, deer and paddles from the earliest carvings. Weapons and horses appear on later carvings. One scene shows livestock being loaded onto a large outrigger canoe about to set sail. Coming or going? Unknown. This is the most concentrated collection of petroglyphs in Hawaii.

 ## PETROGLYPH ADVENTURE

RISK: 1   **ADRENALINE: 2**

Just finding the location is an adventure in and of itself. The Luahiwa petroglyphs are about a mile off Manele Road (Route 440), accessed via unmarked dirt roads through pineapple fields. You are going the right way when you pass near a high voltage shack and below a water tower. The road forks; you go left into a horseshoe curve. Just after the curve, look to your left for big black boulders on the hillside. Bingo! Climb the short distance up the bluff and you're there.

Club Lanai
☎ 808-871-1144 or 800-531-5262
Club Med-style resort on Lanai's very secluded eastern shore. One price includes everything for a full day of fun and relaxation.

Lanai City Service/Dollar Rent Λ Car
Lanai City, HI 96763
☎ 808-565-7227
Rents 4WDs and jeeps for radical excursions.

Ed Robinson's Diving Adventures
PO Box 616
Kihei, Lanai, HI 96753
☎ 808-879-3584 or 800-635-1273
Charter scuba diving trips to Cathedrals and other Lanai locations.

Lahaina Divers
710 Front Street
Lahaina, Maui, HI 96761
☎ 808-667-7496
Offers scuba gear rental, instruction and excursions to Lanai.

Lanai-Maui Interisland Ferry
PO Box 1763
Lahaina, Maui, HI 96767
☎ 800-695-2624
Five crossings daily. $25 each way, bicycles $10 extra. Reservations strongly advised.

Lanai Voyage of Discovery
☎ 808-848-6360 or 800-852-4183
From Maui, circumnavigate Lanai abroad the double-hulled Navatek II. *Meals and snorkeling gear included.*

Ocean Riders
☎ 808-661-3586
Adventure raft trip around Lanai. Includes meals and snorkeling.

Spinning Dolphin Charters
PO Box 491
Lanai City, Lanai, HI 96763
☎ 808-565-9913
Half-day and full-day fishing, snorkeling and whale-watching in season.

Trilogy Ocean Sports
Manele Bay Hotel
Lanai City, Lanai, HI 96763
☎ 808-661-4743
Offers PADI certification courses, rentals and dive excursions.

MOLOKAI

"The windward coast of Molokai is gloomy and abrupt. A wall of cliff two to three thousand feet in height extends the more part of the length (some forty miles) from east to west." ~ Robert Lewis Stevenson, *Travels in Hawaii,* 1889

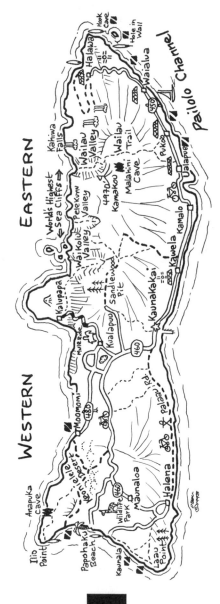

Just like Robert Lewis Stevenson, visitors to Molokai are blown away by the immense cliffs on the back side. These *pali* are the highest sea cliffs in the world. This is where the opening scenes from *Jurassic Park* were shot. Above the *pali*, the lush mountains on the East End host one of the last spots where sandalwood trees grow, but they are very hard to find. Secluded waterfalls, abundant wildlife, and deserted trails scatter across the eastern rain-soaked mountains. Molokai is Hawaii preserved, and in that context, extreme adventures pervade the island.

Molokai is the fifth largest island in Hawaii, measuring a modest 260 square miles. It was created by three volcanoes marking its present geographic regions. The youngest is on the **East End**, where the rugged sea cliffs top off at the 4,970-foot Mount Kamakou; another region is the **West End**, where the arid Mauna Loa flatland rises only 1,380 feet; the last is the low and flat **Kalaupapa Peninsula**, which was the result of a late-forming eruption. Each region offers something totally different. Kalaupapa Peninsula is accessible only by hiking, mountain biking or mule riding down the precarious *pali*. The West End so much resembles the African Savannah that the Molokai Ranch Wildlife Park has simulated that scene, complete with giraffes, antelopes, ostriches, and zebra. Some of the longest and least-visited beaches in Hawaii are found on Molokai's western shoreline.

The best thing about a visit to Molokai is how remote it feels. Once known as "The Lonely Isle" because so few natives inhabited it, Molokai is still pretty sparse as far as population goes. No more than 7,000 souls live here today, most of whom are pure-blooded Hawaiian. Without a single stoplight or elevator on the island and no building taller than a palm tree, it's the remoteness of Molokai that makes it so appealing. Strange that Molokai, sandwiched between the two mega-tourist destinations of Maui and Oahu, manages to keep its slow and traditional pace. This easy-going lifestyle certainly shows in the people, thus earning the island its new nickname: "The Friendly Isle."

BIKING ACROSS THE ISLAND

Bicycle riding across Molokai has become increasingly popular, especially with day-trippers coming over from Maui on the *Princess*. Road traffic is slow-going and light, making it ideal for bicyclists. The roads are all pretty good, but you will come across an occasional pothole, especially out east near Halawa. Mountain bikers relish the dirt tracks on the gently rolling and mostly flat western side. Strong winds sometimes make for hard work. Due to prickly plants, mountain bikers should always carry a tube repair kit and a pump.

For ease, especially for those coming over for a day, all trips start at **Kaunakakai**, the capital and port town. The capital is nothing but dusty streets and falsefront stores. It's a good place to stock up on supplies. Bicycles may be rented in the capital at **Molokai Bicycles** (no telephone) on Mohala Street in downtown Kaunakakai. Some of the fish and surf rental shops also have a few bikes to rent, as does **Fun Hogs**

Hawaii, ☎ 808-552-2555. Just ask around for whatever you need. Remember, this is the friendly island!

Along the Molokai coast.

FROM CAPITAL TO PAPOHAKU BEACH

 RISK: 3   ADRENALINE: 3

Papohaku Beach is one of the largest and most beautiful beaches in the state – and one of the least visited. Those who make it out this far are rewarded with pristine white sand beaches and surrounding sand dunes for their exclusive pleasures. Run around naked if you like! Riding to and from Papohaku takes a good full day, so watch your time if you plan on taking the ferry back. Those sticking to the roads can get here quickest on Kaluakoi Road from Route 460. Mountain bikers can ride almost the whole way on dirt and gravel tracks along the coast. Some of the dirt roads are blocked by gates on Molokai Ranch's private land, and are officially off-limits. If you have a good sense of direction, just figure it out – it's totally doable.

FROM CAPITAL TO KALAUPAPA

RISK: 8   ADRENALINE: 6

Another ride seriously frowned upon, and pretty difficult, is the steep grade down to Kalapapa Peninsula. For one, mountain bikes scare the shit out of mules. Two, the peninsula is only to be visited with a pre-reserved ticket for an official park tour. If you are willing to try it with risk of being kicked out at any given moment, be aware that there are no guard rails to save you. Take the descent very slowly, the cliff walls are sheer and to fall over would mean certain death. The ride back up is tough, mainly because there are so many wooden log-steps to bounce over.

FROM CAPITAL
TO HALAWA

RISK: 2

ADRENALINE: 5

The road from Kaunakakai to Halawa is narrow and sometimes winding, but rarely crowded. Any shortcomings the road might have are compensated for by the outstanding views. Toward the sea you look across a narrow channel at the islands of Maui and Lanai. Inland are the steep green mountain slopes topped by Mount Kamakou. Along the shoreline, notice all the ancient fish ponds; some are said to have been built personally by early Hawaiian kings. A few of the fish ponds are perfectly preserved, but many were partially destroyed by the 1946 tidal wave. Just off the road on the mountain side are several *heiaus*, including Molokai's own City of Refuge: *Kawela Pu'uhonua*. All are nothing more than big piles of volcanic rock, and can be difficult to locate unless you have a friendly local show you the way.

HALAWA VALLEY

Route 450 ends at the tiny village of Halawa, after passing over a prominent ridge with breathtaking views. Halawa Valley once had many times more than its present population. The 1946 *tsunami* killed some inhabitants and most of the survivors decided to relocate to higher ground. There is ample evidence in the valley of building foundations from its bustling days, as well as some Polynesian artifacts. Please don't take anything but photographs.

 ## WATERFALLS HIKE
RISK: 7   ADRENALINE: 5

The hike up the valley to the falls is not far, only a two-hour hike each way. **Hipuapua Falls** and **Moaula Falls** are clearly visible from Halaw. The main problem is that some of the locals own portions of the trail and have fenced off certain sections, making it difficult to reach the falls. The State is trying to negotiate an open trail deal but, until they do, you may have to climb a fence and deal with some not-so-friendly locals. It's worth a try though – the Moaula pool is like swimming in champagne with the force of the falls making the pool's surface a playground of bubbles.

OTHER PALI ADVENTURES

The name of the game is to spend as much time as possible near the *pali*. Whether it's flying alongside in a helicopter or chartered plane, taking a kayak or boat outing, or hiking in the hard way, these majestic cliffs are not to be missed. Some excursions require serious physical stamina and careful preparation. For starters, dress to get dirty.

WAILAU VALLEY TREK

RISK: 9　　　*ADRENALINE: 6*　

Bushwhacking through miles of overgrown trails is the name of the game on this excursion. Here is one of the roughest hikes in Hawaii. Be prepared to hike 10 hours each way in muddy rainforest conditions. The trail extends clear across the island from north to south, and was the native's route for bringing back volcanic rocks used in *heiau* construction. Today it is a jungle with wild boar and treacherous trails. The trail leading down the 3,000-foot cliff is steep and tricky, heavily wooded, and overgrown. The reward is the five-mile-long and one-mile-wide Wailau Valley. This magical spot drains over a hundred waterfalls and is one of the most remote places in all of Hawaii. Locate the trailhead off route 450 about 15 miles east of Kaunakakai, or call Walter Naki (☎ 808-558-8184) for the best guided tour available.

KAYAK TO PELEKUNU VALLEY

RISK: 7   ADRENALINE: 9

Experienced ocean kayakers are able to explore isolated valleys and remote hideaways better than anyone else. Summer is ideal when the water is flat. Winter can be outright dangerous. Put in your kayaks at Halawa and set out on an epic voyage. Pelekunu is another valley completely sealed-off from the rest of Molokai. All these secluded valleys once held substantial populations in pre-contact times. Now they are yours to discover with only the occasional helicopter overhead to keep you company. Pelekunu has a trail leading up the valley, and some expert climbers have navigated the overgrown trail out to the top.

WAIKOLU & PELEKUNU VALLEY OVERLOOK TRAILS

RISK: 5   ADRENALINE: 5

There is a 4WD track called Maunahui Road leading up to the Waikolu lookout, some 3,700 feet above the spectacular green valley. The dirt road never gets super steep, and can be done on a mountain bike. Past Waikolu lookout begins the Kamakou Preserve and the **Hanalilolilo Trail**, which makes its way through some really bizarre high-altitude swamps. This connects to the **Pepe'opae Trail**, where the boardwalk leads you over marshland to another mind-blowing lookout, this time over the north coast and Pelekunu Valley. Round-trip can easily be done in a day.

KALUPAPA PENINSULA TRIPS

Kalupapa was once a place of immeasurable human suffering, lessened only by one man named Father Damien who submitted his life to ease the pain of others. To understand the true anguish of the lepers, consider this description by Robert Lewis Stevenson, reflecting on his visit to Kalupapa in the late 19th century: "They were strangers to each other, collected by common calamity, disfigured, mortally sick, banished without sin from home and friends. Few would understand the principle on which they were thus forfeited in all that life holds dear; many must have conceived their ostracism to be grounded in malevolent caprice; all came with sorrow at heart, many with despair and rage. In the chronicle of man there is perhaps no more melancholy landing than this of the leper immigrants among the ruined houses and dead harvests of Molokai."

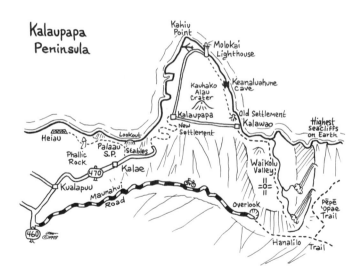

SNEAKING INTO
WAIKOLU VALLEY

RISK: 8

ADRENALINE: 7

Although leprosy as a disease is gone from the peninsula, there are a few dozen cured, former patients still living there. An arrangement with the State allows outsiders to enter with permission from a local, or to take the kinda-sappy guided tour (which does not include Waikolu Valley). Once in Kalupapa (new settlement), the official tour is supposed to be the only way to see the peninsula; no independent exploring allowed. Sneaking in is tough, and the risk is a $500 fine from a State official. But since most residents are now senior citizens and there are rarely State officials down there, the crafty will arrive unseen and feign ignorance if caught. Adventure over – back the way you came. The fortunate few head straight for the unbelievably beautiful and sacred Waikolu Valley, a lush tropical virgin wilderness at its finest.

MULE RIDE TO KALAUPAPA
RISK: 2   ADRENALINE: 4

So you don't want to do the solo-exploration-sneak-in-thing. That's okay. The fewer, the better. The next best way to experience Kalaupapa is by the world-famous mule ride, which is a total blast! Saddle up at the 1,664-foot lookout and descend three miles on picturesque switchback trails. Once on the valley floor you will take the half-day tour out to the old settlement, which is quite interesting and informative the first time around. The mules go back up the same day and reach the top before sunset. It's pretty hilarious watching everyone get off the mules and walk like Alice in the Grand Canyon episode from the Brady Bunch!

★

HORSEBACK RIDING

Molokai Ranch, the West End ranch that covers more than a third of the island, offers half-day and multi-day horseback ride excursions. Perhaps the most popular outing is the two-hour ride to a secluded beach on the western shore. You stop to swim, snorkel and kayak before heading back. The

Molokai Ranch also offers accommodations, meals and a number of other activities. If you choose to stay there, you can take a saddle tour out to the working ranch and interact with the *paniolos* (Hawaiian cowboys). See *Outfitters & Resources* for details. Another company, **Molokai Wagon Ride** (☎ 558-8380 or 567 6773) offers the same package, as well as guided horseback tours of the eastern side.

WINDSURFING PAILOLO CHANNEL TO MAUI

This is an extreme adventure that completely exceeds the Risk and Adrenaline Meters in this book: 10-plus in both categories. Only world-class sailboarders should even *think* about it. Stop! Get that thought out of your mind! Oh, you've sailed the big waves at Hookipa? You understand strong ocean currents and wind patterns? You can sail for 16 miles and four hours straight? Then rig-up for one of the most exciting ocean crossings in Hawaii! The constant wind in the Pailolo Channel will definitely get you to Maui, but will your stamina and skill make it? Sailors have reported seeing humpback whales, dolphins, pilot whales, and even large sharks in the crossing. These are the least of your worries if you go down. The currents in the Pailolo Channel are some of the strongest in the state and can wash you out into the open sea very quickly. Do, or quite literally, die.

SNORKELING MOLOKAI

Excellent locations for snorkeling and scuba shore dives are scattered about the island. Most sites are secluded and untrammeled without the hordes of tourists so common on the other islands. There are a couple of outfitters on Molokai that rent equipment and lead boat dives. These same companies also offer kayak excursions, fishing outings, sailing trips, and PADI certification (see *Outfitters & Resources*).

The best snorkeling and scuba spots on the East End are Fagans, Murphy (at Mile Marker 20), Honouli Wai, Honouli Maloo and Sandy. On the West End, try Kaupoa, Kapukahehu, Moomomi, Poolau, and Kaunala. Precise directions to each location can be obtained in the rental shops.

WARNING...

Never wade or snorkel in the fish ponds. Here reside huge crabs with claws big enough to snip off a toe!

DIVING MOKUHO'ONIKI ROCK

Off the far eastern tip of Molokai is an exceptional dive site known as Mokuho'oniki Rock. This bird sanctuary was once a bombing target island in WWII, and artifacts have been sighted on rare occasions. However, most expeditions come to witness the dramatic drop-offs and unusual marine life. Hammerhead sharks, eagle rays, large jacks, barracuda, and manta rays frequent the depths surrounding the rock. Some outfitters from Maui make the channel crossing on calm days.

HOLE IN THE WALL
& HOOK COVE

 RISK: 6   ADRENALINE: 4

Both locations at Mokuho'oniki Rock are boat dives for advanced divers only. Currents are exceptionally strong in certain places. The reward of both sites is the exceptional wide variety and abundance of sea creatures. Hole in the Wall is a series of ledges and ridges harboring vast amounts of schooling fish trying to stay out of the current. Hook Cove is a semi-circular bowl in about 40 feet of water where schools of tropical fish swim in unison. Over the edge, the drop-off begins. This is where most of the big animals reside. Hook Cove is an excellent night dive, with an incredible assortment of nocturnal creatures not visible in the day, including abundant lobsters.

Outfitters & Resources

Air Molokai
☎ 808-553-3638
Scenic airplane tours by knowledgeable locals. Flights go around the island, as well as stopping in Kalaupapa.

Bill Kapuni's Snorkel and Dive
☎ 808-553-9867
Follow native Hawaiian Bill as you dive and snorkel the best of Molokai's spots. Certification courses and rentals available.

Chris's Bike Adventures
☎ 808-871-BIKE
Ride the best sites of Molokai on a bike. Breakfast and lunch included.

Fun Hogs Hawaii
Kaluakoi Hotel and Golf Club
☎ 808-552-2555
Rents camping gear, mountain bikes and dive equipment. Also offers kayak, snorkeling, catamaran and mountain bike excursions.

Ma'a Hawaii (Molokai Action Adventures)
PO Box 1269
Kaunakakai, Molokai, HI 96748
☎ 808-558-8184
Native Hawaiian Walter Naki leads action adventures on Molokai, including hunting feral axis deer, wild boar and goats. Hunters may use a crossbow or rifle. Walter also leads hikes, and fishing and diving excursions.

Molokai Snorkel & Scuba
PO Box 1962
Kaunakakai, Molokai, HI 96748
☎ 808-553-9867
Rents snorkeling and fishing gear. Directions and excursions to the island's best spots.

Molokai-Maui Interisland Ferry
☎ 808-553-5736 or 800-833-5800
Morning departure, evening return. No charge for bikes.

Molokai Mule Ride
Box 200
Kaunakakai, Molokai, HI 96757
http://www.muleride.com
☎ 800-567-7550
8:20 am departure on a three-mile mule-back excursion down 1,700 feet to the Kalaupapa Peninsula.

Molokai Ranch

http://molokai-ranch.com

☎ 800-254-8871

Owners of a working ranch covering more than a third of the island have now entered the tourism business. Horseback excursions, mountain bikes, kayak outings and accommodations.

Molokai Wagon Ride

☎ 808-558-8380 or 567-6773

A fun day rolling along secluded beaches in a wagon. Run by locals who keep the group fully entertained.

Papillon Helicopters

☎ 800-367-7095

From Maui, fly to the backside of Molokai and experience the world's tallest seacliffs.

OΔHU

"This climate; these voyagings; these landfills at dawn; new islands peaking from the morning bank; new forested harbors; new passing alarms of squalls and surf; new interests of gentle natives— the whole tale of my life is better to me than any poem." ~ Robert Lewis Stevenson, Letters From Honolulu, 1889

Oahu is rich in culture and history, and is every bit as beautiful as the other islands, albeit more crowded. Oahu is only the third biggest island in the chain, but it is home to three-quarters of a million people, or about 80% of the total population of Hawaii. Although this is the land of aloha, Oahu was the site of a bloody battle fought during King Kamehameha's 1795 conquest of the Hawaiian Islands. The battle started near present-day Honolulu and the defenders were pressed into a dead-end valley. From the Nu'uanu Pali Lookout 11 miles outside of Honolulu, you have not only a spectacular view of the windward side, but also of the towering cliff where hundreds of defeated Oahuans fell to their death.

Oahu is known by many monikers: "The Gathering Place," "The Aloha Island," "The Capital Isle," and the "Heavenly Homeland of the North" by early Polynesians. Whatever you want to call it, Oahu offers much more than the rampant commercialization of Waikiki and Honolulu. And extreme adventures abound.

Whatever you do, get out of the city ASAP. From Waikiki, travel east to the windward coast, past mile after mile of incredible beaches or bays. Jungles and waterfalls teem on this rain-soaked side, and hang gliders take it all in after launching from Makapuu's 1,200-foot cliffs. Get to the north coast for some of the world's most famous surf breaks at Waimea Bay, Sunset Beach and the Banzai Pipeline. To the west of the Waianae Range on the leeward side of the island, enjoy secluded beaches and some fantastic diving.

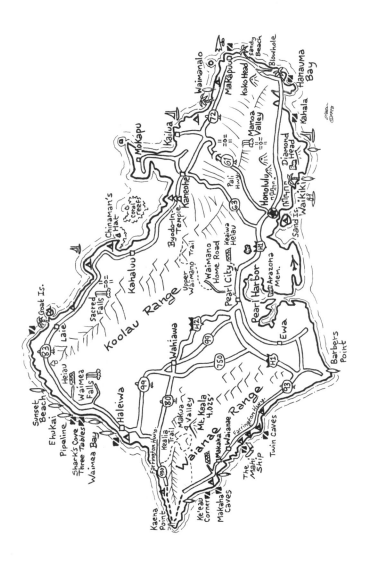

SURF LEGEND

Surfing is no stranger to Hawaiian locals. In fact, the sport was invented by them. One of the earliest descriptions of surfing, written by Captain Cook crew member James King in 1779, is as follows: ".... The men lay themselves flat upon an oval piece of plank... they wait the time for the greatest swells that sets on shore, and altogether push forward with their arms to keep on its top. It sends them in with a most astonishing velocity..." Balancing on a slim board and skimming the crest of a 30 mph breaker must have seemed very odd to the first Western visitors.

In olden times surfing was considered a royal game governed by an exacting ritual. For it was not only a test of skill and athletic ability; it was the chosen sport of kings and queens, and they undertook it only with the help of their gods. The best beaches on all the islands were reserved for the kings and queens of Hawaii. At Waikiki there are still sections of the beach called Queen's Surf and King's Surf as memorials to those times. Ancient surfing contests would draw royalty and commoners to the beach where they would gamble recklessly on the outcome of events. A man could lose everything – his house, his wife, even his own freedom – if he backed the wrong rider. The thrill of looming danger must have been equal to surfer and observer alike.

When the Christian missionaries moved in, they quickly put a stop to the heathen and hectic game. It was not revived until the early 20th century by surf legend Duke

Kahanamoku, who wisely reintroduced surfing as purely a sport of game and skill. Duke was the most celebrated turn-of-the-century "Beach Boy," who, as an Olympic diving and swimming champion, toured the world demonstrating surf techniques. Duke is largely credited for introducing the sport of surfing to the world, and there is a big statue of him right on the central stretch of Waikiki Beach.

SURFING PIPELINE & THE NORTH SHORE

The north shore of Oahu is indisputably the most famous – and most hairball – surf location in the world. From November through February some of the biggest surfable waves on the planet come pounding in here. Places like Sunset Beach, Ehukai, Banzai Pipeline, Waimea Bay and Haleiwa Beach are for expert surfers only. Others may be risking their lives. The summer, however, is a completely different story, when even beginner surfers can handle the waves.

SURFING THE NORTH SHORE ON A WINTER SWELL

RISK: 9 ADRENALINE: 10

If you've surfed the big boys before, get ready for the adrenaline jolt of your life! Nothing on the Hawaiian Islands can compare to the excitement, or life-threatening risk, of riding a big wave on the north shore. Pull it off and you'll join the elite rank of top surfers who can say they've survived. Don't pull it off, and, well, hope you had a good life.

OTHER OAHU BREAKS

The north shore is not the only place to ride a surfboard in Oahu, just the most notorious. Great surf breaks surround the island, and there's one foe every skill level – from beginner waves all the way up to swells for the expert who's not quite crazy enough to surf the north shore after a winter storm. Many of the advanced breaks are considered "Local's Only." This means if you paddle out and a pack of men tell you to get the #@%&*! out of the water, it's best to heed their warning. It never hurts to try and befriend the pack, as a way to avoid a fight.

Unfortunately, surfing in Oahu is sometimes very territorial. This said, here are a few of the most notable breaks. On the leeward Waianae Coast, try Makaha Beach Park north of Makaha town, or Yokohama Bay, even farther north. Less hairball spots on the Leeward Coast are Pupukea Beach Park and Ehukai Beach Park. Along the southern windward coast is Waimanalo Beach Park for nice gentle breakers. On the south coast is Kalaeloa, or Barber's Point, as well as some obvious spots around Waikiki.

WWii FORTRESS, DiAMOND HEAD

Make your way to the entrance of **Diamond Head State Monument** and through a tunnel in the northeast rim of the cone to the parking lot. Here, the trail starts behind the restrooms and makes its way through dusty strands of *koa haole* on the floor of the cone. Soon you will come upon a steep trail leading up to the rim of the cone. The trail roughly follows the contour of the cliff's rim before climbing up another cliff face.

DIAMOND HEAD BUNKERS
RISK: 4   ADRENALINE: 4

It's a good idea to bring a flashlight because there are quite a few old batteries you can get into and explore. The first bunker you reach is past a dark tunnel in a big dark room. Here you will find a spiral staircase leading up to a pillbox through which spotters once watched and wide guns poked out. The slot is wide enough to climb through, and now you will be rewarded with some of the best views in Oahu at the nearby viewing platforms.

From this area you will notice other bunkers and trails which are blocked off. If you're feeling frisky, jump the fence and stay on the rim trail to some of these other fortresses. Most will be locked, but there is usually a way to get into them. The sites ring the rim of Diamond Head and, with some bushwhacking and determination, you can make it all the way around.

TREKKING THE KOOLAU & WAIANAE RANGES

Perhaps the best way to discover the crest of the spectacular Koolaus is via the popular but strenuous Upper Waimano Adventure. This 14-mile trek gains nearly 2,000 feet in elevation and takes a full day to complete. The best thing about this trek is that the hike starts on the leeward side of Oahu, and takes you up and up to the crest of the Koolaus for awesome views of the windward Oahu side.

UPPER WAIMANO ADVENTURE

RISK: 2

ADRENALINE: 5

Getting to the trailhead is not too hard. Take H1 to the Pearl City exit (Exit 10) and get off on Moanalua Road then drive northwest. When you reach Waimano Home Road, turn right, and follow the road 22¼ miles until you reach a fence surrounding Waimano Home. Park in the dirt lot on the left near the fence and start your hike. The trail forks to the left and right (Lower and Upper trails). Stay right and follow the old irrigation trail among ferns and thick Christmas berry thickets.

As the trail winds its way further into the jungle and towards the mountains, keep a lookout for mango, guava, mountain apple, and wild ginger. The trail basically parallels Waimano Stream, through a dramatic valley and along the irrigation channel and (usually) dry streambed. After rounding the nose of a small ridge, a switchback sends you up through some exotic trees until you are high above the valley. The views are amazing from here on out. The best comes – you'll be pleasantly surprised – when you cross the ridge and behold the windward side of Oahu.

Unfortunately, the trail ends near here. Any attempt to go further can be extremely dangerous, so you'll have to retrace your steps and go back the way you came.

KEALIA TRAIL IN THE WAIANAE RANGE

 RISK: 2   **ADRENALINE: 3**

The only designated hike in the Waianae Range is the Kealia Trail on the northern end of the mountains. This half-day hike takes you through a dry forest on a switchback trail up, up and up for an elevation gain of 2,000 feet. The trail climaxes with a dramatic overlook of Makua Valley on the southeast side of the range, as well as a view of Mount Kaala. The hearty hiker can carry on to the leeward side for a full-day hike around the spectacular Kaena Point.

Access to the Kealia Trail begins on the windward side of Oahu off Highway 930, a.k.a. the Farrington Highway. This trail starts in the Dillingham Airfield, which offers free parking, but closes at sunset. Inside the airfield, travel to the west end and pass through a gate. Bear to the left for a third of a mile until you reach a rough-paved area. Here the trail begins behind the airfield and up the Dillingham Cliffs. A series of switchbacks on the dirt road lead you up through interesting vegetation until you reach a plateau. This is a confusing trail, there are many unmarked forks. Make sure you take all left forks. Continue ascending and you will eventually make it to a lofty knoll overlooking Makua Valley. Only by studying a good topography map can you navigate this route successfully. It is difficult from the lookout to Kaena Point. Serious trekkers can continue to the top of 4,025-foot Mount Kaala by following the Dupont Trail.

KAENA POINT

The rugged and windswept Kaena Point is an excursion not to be missed. Here on Oahu's far northwest shore you will find the tail-end of the Waianae Range, as well as the confluence of two distinct weather systems – the leeward and windward. The ocean currents meet in a constant splash of dark water and white foam on jagged rocks. Kaena Point is the nesting ground of many rare Hawaiian birds, including the immense Laysan albatross, who may take to the air to drive you away from their nests if you venture too close. Make your way out to the lighthouse for splendid views, and maybe even a ghost. Hawaiian legend tells us this is the place where recently deceased souls come before their journey to heaven or hell.

Kaena Point may be reached from both the windward (northwest) and leeward (southwest) sides. The old dirt road used to be open for 4WD traffic, but time and erosion have closed it. Both access points are on the Farrington Highway. Old maps may show this road rounding Kaena Point, and indeed it does, but there is no way any vehicle can make it past some of the deep erosion trenches. All the better. Look for the parking lots where the pavement ends, Mile Marker 42 on the leeward side – Mile Marker 46 on the windward side.

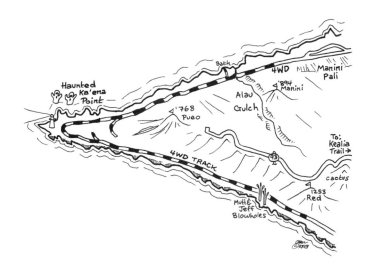

KAENA POINT EXCURSIONS

RISK: 3   ADRENALINE: 4

The 10-mile stretch of dirt road rounding Kaena Point has become an increasingly popular trip for naturalists, hikers, and mountain bikers. There are actually 20 or 30 miles of trails if you include all the unmapped side-routes. Several side trails lead to remote beaches, blowholes, and exceptional viewing areas along the coast. Mountain bikers will have to dismount to get around ditches or deep sand dunes on the windward side, but they have the advantage of being able to explore more side-trails in a day than a hiker could. Diving and snorkeling is generally best on the dry and rocky leeward side, while the vegetation and cliffs are more interesting on the windward side. But why limit yourself? Pack up your snorkeling gear and a lunch and set out for a great day on both sides!

DiVE SiTES OF OAHU

Turtles draw a crowd in the Canyon.

TURTLE CANYON & HANAUMA BAY

RISK: 2   ADRENALINE: 3

On the southeastern shore of Oahu are several bays just made for snorkelers and scuba divers. The first is Maunalua Bay, popularly called Turtle Canyon after the large number of sea turtles that make this their home. Divers can expect to see five to 10 turtles at any given time hanging out on the sandy floor or in reef depressions. The turtles are quite accustomed to seeing people and are not easily scared, so photographing them is easy. No spectacular lava or coral formations at Turtle Canyon, but it's teeming with various aquatic creatures. Shore dives are difficult, so most adventurers opt to take a boat.

Oahu's most renowned snorkeling spot is Hanauma Bay – only a 20-minute drive from Waikiki. This beautiful bay is actually an extinct volcano, formed when the outer wall gave way to the sea. Hundreds of tourists flock here every day, so diving is best in the early morning. Scuba divers will look really cool suiting up on the beach and flopping out past the snorkelers in the Inner Reef. Access the Outer Reef by following the large cable through a channel. This will open to 50-70 feet of water, but head to the right side of the bay to Palea Point. Down below the point is a great wall. If the current is strong, head back. Outside the bay is Witch's Brew, named for the strong waves and currents that merge here. On a calm day you can drop down to a lush coral reef which is home to countless interesting sea critters.

 ## NORTH SHORE DIVES
RISK: 5 ADRENALINE: 4

North shore dives are safe only from May to October when the winter swells die down.

This area can be very dangerous during periods of medium to high surf, especially for cave divers, so wait until the water is flat in the summer. Snorkelers and scuba divers alike enjoy the easy beach access of north shore dives, as well as the great formations and abundant marine life.

Perhaps the most highly regarded north shore dive is **Shark's Cove**, located at Pupukea Beach Park off coast road 83. Suit-up for this dive on the small sandy beach, then proceed to swim around the point on the far right of the bay. Dropping down, you will find a nice wall with plenty of caves, arches, and lava tubes to explore. Shark's Cove is also a great snorkel and night dive location.

Less than one mile southeast of Shark's Cove is another fine snorkel/scuba site called **Three Tables**. The recognizable three flat lava shelves that give the site its name can be seen from the road. Drop-in from the rocky shoreline in front of the parking lot, or from the small sandy beach. There are good lava formations directly offshore, but most divers head to the right of the beach for the maze of lava tubes and archways.

MAKAHA CAVES & KE'EAU CORNER

RISK: 3 **ADRENALINE: 4**

The Makaha Caves and Ke'eau Corner are quite close to one another. Both are located off Oahu's western shore. These two sites are usually paired up as a double boat dive, yet each offers an entirely different scuba experience. Makaha Caves, as the name suggests, offers up lava caverns as well as grottoes, ledges, archways and overhangs for interesting exploration. Because Makaha is relatively shallow (20-45 feet), and because the caves offer many escape routes, this site is ideal for first-timers and night divers.

Ke'eau Corner is the extension of the wall you see at Makaha Caves. It extends all the way to Ke'eau Beach Park. Most boats anchor at a point that gives access to the most spectacular part of the wall, including massive holes, arches, and pinnacles. Sea life is abundant here, as it is at Makaha Caves. The current is normally very light, allowing boat divers a no-stress wall dive, and strong swimmers can access this site from the beach. The whole of Oahu's leeward coast is ideal for snorkelers.

DIVING THE SUNKEN WRECK MAHI

 RISK: 6   **ADRENALINE: 7**

The finest wreck dive in Hawaii is also one of the most popular underwater attractions on Oahu. The *Mahi* is a 165-foot minesweeper intentionally sunk in 1983 to create an artificial reef. The ship is fully intact, resting upright in 95 feet of water. She can be found a mile offshore on the leeward side of the island, near Maili Point. All dives must be made from a boat.

When the seas are calm, divers can enter the wreck from several different approaches. All three of the lower decks are open for exploration, as is the pilothouse.

> **TIP**
>
> It is very important for divers to stay away from the bottom of the ship so they do not stir up silt and lose visibility.

In and around the wreck are schools of colorful fish, lobsters, reef sharks, and the occasional manta or eagle ray. Off the port side of the *Mahi* lies another wreck – a large barge. When visibility exceeds 100 feet, which it usually does, the barge is clearly seen. Only experienced divers should attempt to swim over, and only when there is little or no current. Another deep dive nearby is an area called Twin Caves.

BEACH ACTIVITIES

So you're stuck in Waikiki and wondering what there is to do? Don't fret. Just about any watersport or beach activity you can dream of is at your disposal. A short stroll along the beach and you will soon discover volleyball games, surfboard rentals, canoe excursions, kayak rentals, windsurf gear, boogie boards, jet skis, snuba, scuba and snorkeling gear. Activity desks in the hotels and discount booths on the streets can arrange your helicopter ride, dive trip, horseback ride, parasail experience, waterski outing, bicycle or moped rental. Don't worry about finding these activity salespeople – they'll find you.

In the fine tradition of Hawaiian royalty, our favorite Waikiki extreme adventure is to rent a catamaran and sail out on the bay. The double-hulled outrigger canoe was introduced by the early Polynesians, and a sail off Waikiki Beach on a modern catamaran could bring back some of those memories. You also might want to check with the **Outrigger Canoe Club**, a shack on the beach (no telephone); they sometimes let walk-ons work out with the team. Tell them you've paddled before and would be honored if you could join them. That would be an authentic experience in this land of the artificial.

GOAT ISLAND

Many regard **Malaekahana State Recreation Area** near the town of Laie as one of the islands' finest parks. This is perhaps the best legal campground on the island, certainly the best on the windward coast. It is isolated from the highway by shady trees. Visitors to the recreation area have a nice beach, nearby diving (between Laie and Laniloa Point), as well as a classic Indiana Jones-style trip out to Goat Island.

 ### GOAT ISLAND EXCURSION
RISK: 2   ADRENALINE: 3

Goat Island, known as Mokuauia Island by Hawaiians, can be accessed only by wading over; best at low tide. On calm days the water is only knee-deep, on rough days it is waist-deep. Goat Island is one of the best "non-official" campgrounds on Oahu, which makes wading over with gear even more exciting. The white sand beach on the leeward side of this bird refuge is a dream South Pacific getaway.

CAMPING

There are a lot of places like Goat Island where you can camp without fees or supervision. The more remote, the better. Usually the give-away is where you park your car. If you don't have one, no problem. Just the same, camping is free in the state and county parks. The hassle is obtaining the necessary permit (Room 310, 1151 Punchbowl Street, Honolulu, HI 96813). See the tent icons on the Oahu map for best locations.

PEARL HARBOR EXCURSION

The **USS Arizona** Memorial in Pearl Harbor is unlike any other sightseeing attraction on the island. The hull of the USS Arizona is the tomb of 1,102 men who perished in Japan's surprise attack on December 7th, 1941. The wreckage can be visited in two ways. The first is aboard an excursion boat that tours the harbor, but can't land at the memorial. The other way is to travel to the visitor's center by land. Ride a bike, drive or catch the #4 shuttle bus from Waikiki, or the #50 city bus. The main bus terminal is in downtown Honolulu at the Ala Moana Center. ☎ 808-848-5555 for schedules and routes. From the visitor's center the navy offers free shuttle boats every half-hour out to the memorial from 7:45 a.m. to 3 p.m. daily. The concrete memorial, built atop the eerie aquatic graveyard, was completed in 1962. Nothing extreme, but very interesting nonetheless.

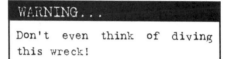

WARNING...

Don't even think of diving this wreck!

CRUISIN' & BOOZIN' AROUND TOWN

Honolulu and Waikiki make up for all the other islands in the nightlife department – though Lahaina, Maui, also has a lot to offer. From famous international bands to traditional entertainers, from hopping discos to the sleaziest dive bar imaginable, there is something for everyone here. Most bars shut down at 2 a.m., but some with a cabaret license can stay open until 4 a.m., just as long as the band continues to play. Here's a few for the extreme partier.

In Honolulu, start downtown at **Sloppy Joe's** in the Aloha Tower Marketplace. As with its twin brother in Key West, pictures of Papa Hemingway cover the walls and live music keeps the place jumpin' in the wee hours. Get here before 8 p.m. to avoid the cover charge. The young and wild crowd heads to **The Fast Zone**, 1154 Fort Street Mall, for live local punk and reggae bands. Drinks are cheap, but so is the appearance of this joint. Out near the university is **Anna Bananas** at 2440 S. Beretania Street. This place has been the rager of choice among college students for almost 30 years. Upstairs is live music and downstairs is where all the heavy drinkers congregate.

If you don't think you can escape Waikiki for a good time, think again. Even in the epitome of commercial tourism there are some cool jaunts to whet your whistle – all within walking distance. Warm-up at the **Irish Rose Saloon** at 227 Lewers Street. It's not really an Irish Pub, but more like a rowdy live music hall with sporting events on the telly. The ultimate meat-market disco is the ultra-gaudy **Maharaja**, 2555 Kuhio Avenue. Oahu's largest dance floor is the size of a small island, so stay close to your partner or you might just go home with a new one. The best dance club in town is **The Jungle**, 311 Lewers Street. Trance out after 10 p.m. to progressive, house and techno blasting from a high-tech sound system. Last is **Duke's Canoe Club**, right on the beach, 2335 Kalakaua Avenue. Live Hawaiian music on the weekends draws a large local crowd. Gotta love the ambiance at Duke's. Don't forget, every hotel in Waikiki and Honolulu has its own bar if you feel like mingling with the tourist set.

Outfitters & Resources

Department of Land & Natural Resources
Division of State Parks
1151 Punchbowl Street, Room 310
Honolulu, Oahu, HI 96813
☎ 808-548-7455
*Camping permits must be obtained in
person at the above address.*

Dive Oahu
3648 Waialae Ave.
Waialae, Oahu, HI 96816
☎ 808-732-2877
Gear rental, instruction and dive excursions.

Go Bananas Hawaii
730 Kapapupu and 98-406 Kam Hwy.
Pearl City, Oahu, HI 96782
☎ 808-484-0606
*Kayak rental, excursions, and instruction.
They also wave skis and other water toys.*

Kailua Sailboard Company
130 Kailua Road
Kailua, Oahu, HI 96734
☎ 808-262-2555
*Windsurf gear rental and instruction. They
also rent boogie boards and kayaks.*

Leeward Dive Center
87-066 Farrington Hwy.
Maili, Oahu, HI 96792
☎ 808-696-3414
Offers gear rental, instruction and dive excursions. Boats leave from Waianae Harbor.

Naish Hawaii
155 A Hamakua Drive
Kailua, Oahu. HI 96734
☎ 808-262-6068
Windsurf gear rental, repair and instruction. Their retail shop sells custom boards and great clothes.

The Bus
☎ 808-848-5555
Route and schedule information.

Waikiki Diving
420 Nahua and 1734 Kalakua Ave.
Waikiki, Oahu, HI 96815
☎ 808-922-7188 or 808-955-5151
Gear rental, instruction and dive excursions.

Windward Boats & Froome Boat Co.
789 Kailua Road at the Pali Hwy.
☎ 808-261-2961
Hobie Cat rental and lessons. Also rents kayaks, power boats and wave skis.

KAUAI

"How shall we account for this nation spreading itself so far over this vast ocean! We find them from New Zealand to the south, to these islands to the north and from Easter Island to the Hebrides;... how much farther is not known..." ~ Captain James Cook, 1778

History was made repeatedly on Kauai, particularly around Waimea Bay. There are traces of the earliest Hawaiian inhabitants found here, and legends and folklore pervade all corners of the island. It was at Waimea Bay in the winter of 1777-1778 that Captain James Cook first set foot on the Hawaiian islands and was received as a god. Cook was only one of many Europeans who tried to claim Kauai on their own country's behalf. On a bluff above the Captain's bay, the Russians came and built a fort to try and gain a Hawaiian foothold in the early 19th century. Waimea was also the scene of the first missionary settlement, sugarcane plantation, and a sandalwood trade that flourished here until the forests were all but denuded of those fragrant trees.

Kauai Island, a 30-minute flight to the northwest of Oahu, is the firstborn of the Hawaiian islands. Because of its advanced age, Kauai has thicker soil and is more verdant than any of the others, hence it's nickname: "The Garden Isle." This is the island that King Kamehameha was never able to subdue by force. But when he died, one of his widows united the kingdom by marrying both the king and prince of Kauai simultaneously. Must have been an interesting threesome on that wedding night!

When Hurricane Iniki devastated the island in 1993, it wasn't clear how long it would take to clean up and rebuild. Roofs of hotels were ripped off, cars hung from trees, all power lines were down, and nearly every window on the island had been blown out. Well, it didn't take more than a few years, and today it is hard to tell the island was ever really thrashed. While many trees and foliage suffered heavy damage and the beaches lost much sand, all of Kauai's natural wonders remain perfectly intact. Behold the dramatic Na Pali Coast and Waimea Canyon – the "Grand Canyon of the Pacific." Crowning Kauai at 5,170 feet is Mount Waialeale (which means rippling water). It draws nearly 500 inches of rain per year, making it the wettest spot on earth.

NA PALI COAST

he Na Pali Coast (and the western end of the north shore) is a rugged and untamed spectacle. Its name means "The Cliffs," and the area is completely inaccessible, except on foot and by water craft. The ancient trail of the natives, called the Kalalau Trail, is still used and is way more popular today than it ever was. This "must-see" trail is world-renowned. The only other way to gaze upon these fabled cliffs is to make an advance reservation for a boat excursion or helicopter ride.

Na Pali Coast.

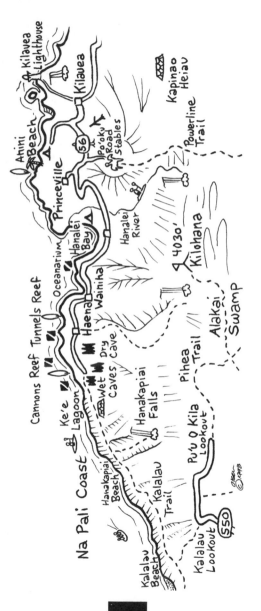

NA PALI DAY HIKE TO
HANAKAPIAI FALLS

RISK: 3   ADRENALINE: 3

Take Highway 56 all the way to its end and park. This is the start of the 11-mile Kalalau Trail, which finishes at the beach of the same name. While Kalalau Beach is much too far to reach in a single hike-in-hike-out day, Hanakapiai Beach is not. It's only two miles to Hanakapiai Beach, and another two to the 300-foot Hanakapiai Falls. The side-trail leading up the steep-walled valley to the falls is not to be missed. These falls are just as exciting as the trail along the Na Pali Cliffs' edge. The Hanakapiai Falls is an eight-mile round-trip that rises 1,750 feet in elevation and takes about five hours. No permit required.

MULTI-DAY
NA PALI TREK

RISK: 5   ADRENALINE: 5

Quite arguably the finest trek in all Hawaii, and most precarious at that, is the 11-mile Kalalau Trail along the Na Pali Coast. This magnificent coastline hike overlooks an endless series of emerald green valleys and steep cliffs, some dropping 3,000 feet to the turbulent sea below. Side-trips lead to various breathtaking waterfalls and secluded beaches. This is not a trek to be rushed. Camping sites are frequent. Just before reaching Kalalau Beach, there is a trail leading inland and up to the Kalalau Lookout. Beyond here, continue trekking to Waimea Canyon and Alakai Swamp.

To hike beyond Hanakapiai Beach requires a camping permit (this is also true for those traveling by boat who wish to land). With so many accidents and injuries on the trails in recent years, the state requires all people staying overnight in Na Pali to be registered. Those wishing to do the multiple-day Na Pali trek are advised to get their permits early. Overall numbers are restricted, and camping sites are limited. Contact the State Parks office at: 3060 Eiwa Street in Lihue, ☎ 808-274-3444. They will also provide an excellent trail map showing all the campsites available.

ADVENTURE RAFTING THE NA PALI COAST

RISK: 2

ADRENALINE: 5

One of the easiest and most rewarding ways to experience the Na Pali Coast is by boat. Many different charters do half-day and full-day snorkeling excursions, but there's only one really extreme boat adventure. Book your trip with one of the few outfitters who offer Zodiac excursions. These highly maneuverable inflatable rafts can zoom in and out of sea caves and race beneath surging waterfalls. Passengers on the other boats can only watch with envy. The down side to a Zodiac is that when the seas become choppy the rides are miserably bumpy and slow-going. Ask about the backpacker drop-off service offered by most operators on their first trip of the day. For the same price as a tour, they will leave you off at Kalalau Beach, where you can begin your Na Pali trek or hike the 11 miles back in a single day.

★

WAIMEA CANYON EXCURSIONS

The Waimea Canyon is a 25-square-mile chasm widely regarded as the most amazing valley in all of Hawaii. Shifting in hue as the day progresses, it displays every shade of green against the rich red earth. Waterfalls, exotic wildlife and rare plants scatter inside and out of the canyon, which measures 10 miles long and one mile wide. There are over 45 miles of networking trails throughout Waimea Canyon and Kokee State Park. Pick up a detailed trail map at any of the state park Ranger Stations. Mark Twain once called Waimea the "Grand Canyon of the Pacific," an apt description. At something just over 3,000 feet, it may not be as deep as its Arizona rival, but the way it fits so compactly into such a small island is nothing short of mind-blowing.

WAIMEA DAY HIKES

RISK: 3

ADRENALINE: 5

If you have only a little while to see Waimea Canyon and still want to get in a quick power hike, there are three good options: top, middle or lower. Take your pick. All allow equally different and spectacular vistas of the multi-colored canyon. The first place to pull over for a look is also the trailhead to the **Kukui Trail**, which starts at the interesting Illiau Nature Loop. Past this vantage point, descend 2,000 feet into the heart of the canyon below, eventually coming out at Wiliwili Camp. Take a dip in the river, spend the night here, or power it back up. The 2.5 miles each way sure seem a lot longer on account of the altitude changes. Allow five hours round-trip.

The shortest journey of the three is also the most refreshing. Midway along Highway 550 is the pull-out for Halemanu Road, a dirt road also suitable for mountain biking. Park here and descend to the **Canyon Trail**, which will then lead you to the spectacular Upper and Lower Waipoo Falls. Upper Waipoo Falls is fronted by a large pool ideal for swimming, while the Lower Falls has showering cascades and smaller pools in which to take a dip. This is pure Tarzan country amid rare birds and native plants. Allow two hours hiking time to do the 3.2-mile round-trip and 600-foot elevation gain.

At the very end of Highway 550 is **Kokee State Park**, where hikers have a number of excellent hiking options. The 3.5-mile **Awaawapuhi Trail** offers unbelievable vistas of the Na Pali Coast. The **Halemanu-Kokee Trail** is a wonderful loop through the upper part of the canyon. But our favorite is the **Pihea Trail** to the Alakai Swamp. While it is hard to see Waimea

Canyon from here, there are excellent views of the Na Pali Coast, as well as some of Hawaii's most bizarre landscapes. The **Alakai Swamp** is the largest wetland area in the state, home to many exotic birds and rare plants. A boardwalk has been erected to protect hikers from mid-thigh mud, but you will still get wet and dirty, so come prepared. It's about a five-hour trek with only slight changes in elevation. Park at Pu'u Lookout, where the Pihea Trail begins.

WAIMEA TOWN TO NA PALI
RISK: 4   ADRENALINE: 6

With the proper camping permits, it is possible to trek the entire length of Kauai – from Waimea town, through the Waimea Canyon to the Alakai Swamp, all the way out to the Na Pali Coast. From Waimea, head up the town road leading to the Menehune Ditch. From here, pick up the **Kekaha Ditch Trail**, which pretty much parallels the Waimea River for several miles. A turnoff from the canyon on to **Kaluahaulu Ridge Trail** leads you to the Waialae Cabin. If you were lucky enough to get reservations for the cabin, you're stylin'. (☎ 808-274-3444.) If not, you can pitch a tent here and, when morning comes, do a side-trip up and back to Kauai's highest mountain, 5,148-foot Mount Waialeale. Mind you, this is the wettest spot on the whole planet, so be prepared to get drenched. After breaking camp at Waialae Cabin, start north on the **Kohua Ridge Trail**, which gets you into the Alakai Swamp region. From here there are several trails and dirt roads to choose from, but if you stay on a general northerly course, you will eventually make it to Highway 550. Locate the Kalalau Lookout and the valley trail down to the famed **Kalalau Trail** along the Na Pali Coast, finishing at Ke'e Beach about a week later.

MOUNTAIN BIKING
WAIMEA CANYON

 RISK: 5 ADRENALINE: 5

On the upper portion of Waimea Canyon are many miles of 4WD dirt roads that are great for extreme mountain biking. These roads can get very muddy, especially the farther east you go towards the rain-catching mountains. You may have to walk around a few mud pits in the road or carry your bike over a rocky creek, so prepare to be covered in red mud. Mountain bikers should park just past the Kokee Museum and Lodge. From here, access Camp 10 Road all the way out to the Alakai Swamp, or turnoff a quarter-way along onto Kumuwela Road. This is some of the best jungle riding in the state. Real mountain biking studs will ride the 16.8 miles from the town of Kekaha. But don't burn yourself out; these extremely exciting tracks require all your energy. Your best bet is to drive a vehicle up with the bikes, saving your energy exclusively for the trails.

BARKING SANDS SIDE-TRIP

While you are on the eastern side of the island, a cool side-trip is out to the remote area of the southern Na Pali known as Barking Sands. It gained its unusual name from the hollow sand grains that squeak, or bark, when you walk on them. The official name is **Polihale Beach and State Park**, which covers 16 long miles of windy beach. Popular activities are dune buggying, windsurfing, and exploring the southern Na Pali cliffs. To get here, travel seven miles past the town of Kekaha and take the right fork past the Pacific Missile Range Facility near Mana. Take a left turn where the sign directs you, and follow the dirt roads all the way to the Polihale day-use parking area. Arrange a camping permit **from the state park office** (☎ 808-274-3444).

SEA KAYAKING THE SOUTHERN NA PALI

RISK: 8

ADRENALINE: 6

Topping the list of extreme adventures, this one requires it all: skill, endurance, preparation and instinct. In the summer months it is possible to kayak the entire length of the Na Pali Coast. By creating your own kayak excursion, you can get to places nobody else goes, namely the Valley of the Lost Tribes, where thousands of natives once lived. Pull up in your boat much the same way they did, and explore virgin jungle valleys – one after the other. Even though there is hardly any way you could get caught, you should still register (☎ 808-274-3444) for a free camping permit and let them know you'll be out there. You never know when someone might get hurt.

NOTABLE DIVE SITES

Kauai has two distinguishable zones for snorkeling and scuba diving: the north and south shores. The north shore is diveable only in the summer after the winter swells simmer down, while the south shore is pretty decent all year round. Being the oldest island in the chain, the underwater lava formations here are more worn, with a smoothed-over look to them. Marine life in Kauai is varied and as abundant as elsewhere in the chain. The following are some of the most popular sites.

CANNONS & TUNNELS REEF

 RISK: 3 ADRENALINE: 4

These two are popular shore dives mainly because of their easy beach access. Both can be reached from Haena Beach Park (Tunnels Beach) on the north shore. Together, they make for the perfect double-dive day. The Cannons are accessed via a trail just west of the park. Look for a cut in the coral reef. This is your way through the reef until you reach a 30-foot wall. Follow the wall to the left where you will reach another drop down to 65 feet, which features a large archway and many caves and holes in the wall.

Tunnels Reef is on the east side of Haena Park, accessed at Mile Marker 36.6 by continuing at the end of a dirt road. Swim out about 30 feet from the shore to a nice drop-off. Experienced divers may follow the boat channel where the slope leads to a series of interconnected lava tubes and chambers in the 50- and 60-foot range. Turtles and (non-dangerous) reef sharks can be spotted on occasion at both sites.

WARNING...

Neither site should be attempted in the winter months when swells and currents are strong. Wait until a calm summer day.

 ## OCEANARIUM

RISK: 7   *ADRENALINE: 6*

Oceanarium is just what the name suggests – a great visibility dive with swarms of tropical fish. It gives the impression of swimming in a giant fish tank. This north shore deep dive is strictly for advanced divers, and accessible only by boat. Three large pinnacles rise to the 70-foot mark, and it's down at the 120-foot level where the great schools of fish reside. Most divers head for the largest of the three pinnacles where a spectacular black coral overhang is home to bright orange tubastraea coral. Quite psychedelic when you're all narced out!

POIPU AREA DIVES

 RISK: 3   ADRENALINE: 4

Popular south shore boat dives include the extreme **Brenneke's Drop-Off** and the **Sheraton Caverns**. Brenneke's is a 90-foot sheer face extending several miles off the southeastern shore. Due to current patterns and the sheer face here, this dive should be attempted only on calm days. Sheraton Caverns, on the other hand, is good almost anytime, barring another hurricane. Named after the resort nearby, the caverns offer nice wide tubes in about 50 feet of water with some super-friendly sea turtles. Koloa Landing is a launching ramp in the town of Poipu often used for training dives because it offers easy access. This also makes the landing popular for night divers.

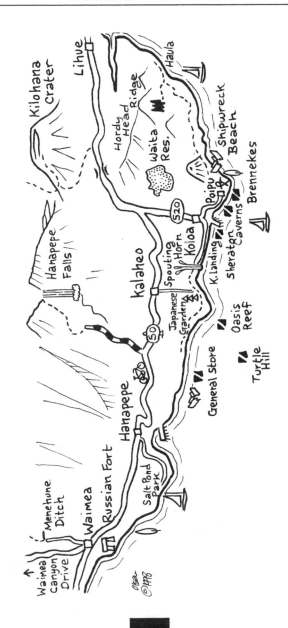

TURTLE HILL & GENERAL STORE

RISK: 5 ADRENALINE: 6

Two good south shore dives are close enough to each other to be done in the same boat outing. Turtle Hill is renowned for, you guessed it, a lot of green sea turtles. To keep the dive exciting, there are a number of caves, ledges and archways to explore alongside your shell-backed swimming friends. The name of General Store comes from the variety of what you can find here, including an 1800's sunken steamship. The wreck is all broken up now, but several large anchors, boilers, and chains can be found. You also have your ever-popular lava tubes, open caverns, interesting coral formations and an abundance of marine life. There's a little bit of everything at the General Store.

WAILUA RIVER ADVENTURES

The Wailua River was once a favorite playground for Hawaiian royalty. In **Lydgate Park**, on Wailua Bay, you can see the remains of *Hauola Pu'uhonua,* a city of refuge once a shelter for anyone escaping from battle or crime. A trail formerly know as the King's Highway once ran from the mouth of the river all the way up to Mount Waialeale, with sacred sites and *heiaus* lining the way. The Wailua River is considered the only navigable waterway in Hawaii, despite sandbars at its mouth preventing vessels from entering via the open sea. The waterway is slow-moving between lush green banks on its course to the ocean – perfect for tropical river adventures.

 ## FERN GROTTO SWIM

RISK: 6   ADRENALINE: 3

This is a favorite Kauaiian extreme adventure – one that requires good swimming abilities, guts, guile, and charm. First, go through Smith's Tropical Paradise (alongside the Wailua River, just off the Kuhio Highway) – a place as kitsch as the Smith tour barges floating to and from the Fern Grotto. At the end of the "tropical paradise" is a sugarcane field. Walk along the dirt roads until you can walk no further. Time to get wet. A three-quarter-mile swim starts here and leads to the Fern Grotto. There are times you can walk along the shore, but most choose to swim the whole way so as not to miss their personal opportunity to moon the tourist barges. When you get there, it's time to use that charm. Certainly at some point someone will ask you what you are doing. "Ummm, swimming to the Fern Grotto? Auditioning for the next Indiana Jones film?" Be creative, you're going to get kicked out anyhow. On your swim back, cross the river at the replicated Hawaiian Village. Here you can hike up a trail which leads to an overlook of the Opaikaa Falls and a road back to Wailua Bay.

RIVER KAYAK TO WAILUA FALLS

 RISK: 3   ADRENALINE: 5

An equally enjoyable way to navigate the river (without fear of reprimand) is to rent a kayak and explore all the branches of the Wailua River. One branch takes you to Opaikaa Falls, another to a rope-swing, and the widest branch to the Fern Grotto and Wailua Falls. Sometimes, a slight breach of private property is necessary to get the kayaks over shallow rockways or logs, but that's part of the experience. The Huleia Stream, Kalihi Wai River and Hanalei River are other popular river kayak waterways. The best option is to rent a river kayak for half a

day without a guide. Go off on your own –
it's nearly impossible to get lost.

 ## WATERSKI & WAKEBOARD
RISK: 2   ADRENALINE: 3

So you want to attract a little attention near
the heavily touristed mouth of the Wailea
River? There's no better place to
demonstrate your waterskiing abilities in
front of an eager crowd. In fact, this is the
only place in the state to waterski on a flat
river, crowds or no crowds. Rent wakeboards,
waterskis, kneeboards, and a ski boat to pull
you along. Inquire about current rates and
other adventures at the **Kauai Water Ski
and Surf Co.** (see below) down at the
marina. You can't take ski boats out by
yourself.

HELICOPTER RIDES

If you've got a little extra cabbage to kick-down, this is the
way to spend it. Kauai is arguably the most intense island
viewed from the window of a helicopter. As is true of all the

islands, pilots can fly to remote and otherwise inaccessible locations. Unlike the other islands, Kauai has the one-of-a-kind Waimea Canyon and the Na Pali Coast. 'Nuff said?

FULL ISLAND HELICOPTER TOUR

RISK: 1

ADRENALINE: 8

Cruising the airspace over Kauai, you can easily see how it has caught the attention of Hollywood. Action films such as *The South Pacific, Raiders of the Lost Ark, King Kong,* and *Jurassic Park* were filmed here. Even scenes from the opening credits of *Fantasy Island* were shot near Wailua Falls. To quote Mr. Roarke schooling Tattoo; "It is said a man's life can be measured by the dreams he fulfills." Quoting Brad Olsen "If you've made it as far as a helicopter ride over Kauai, you must've fulfilled a few by now." ;-)

OTHER NORTH SHORE ADVENTURES

The north shore of Kauai is an adventure lover's delight. Virtually every Hawaiian activity can be found here, including surfing, boogie boarding, windsurfing, snorkeling, scuba diving, rock climbing, horseback riding, hiking, kayaking... and the list goes on. The north shore's natural scenery is stunning, and so are the beaches. Spend as much time as you can here. Consider coming to live here if you have the chance. See the book *World Stompers* by this author for information on how to travel cheaply around the world. It includes a chapter on how to live and work in Hawaii. (If you have Internet access, visit www.stompers.com.)

THE POWER LINE TRAIL
RISK: 2   ADRENALINE: 3

The Power Line Trail is a wide dirt track following a ridge along the lesser-known interior of Kauai. Visible from it are soaring waterfalls, abundant flowers, as well as ocean and mountain views. The power company maintains the track but anyone is free to mountain bike, horseback ride or hike along peacefully. The 13-mile stretch begins at the end of Po'oku Road near Princeville, and continues all the way to the Keahua Arboretum. Also on Po'oku Road are the **Po'oku Stables**, where you can join an organized horseback journey to the top of Kalihiwai Falls and Hanalei Valley. (See *Outfitters & Resources* below.)

CAVE EXCURSIONS

 RISK: 2   ADRENALINE: 3

The Maniniholo Dry Cave, according to legend, was dug by *menehunes* looking for a supernatural being who had stolen their fish. Waikapalae and Waikanaloa Wet Caves were said to have been made by the fire goddess Pele, who scorched the earth as she was trying to make herself a suitable home.

Across the highway from Haena Beach Country Park, a.k.a. Tunnels Beach, is the **Maniniholo Dry Cave**. This long lava tube penetrates deep into the mountain and was once completely under water. Nothing super radical, but definitely worth a look.

Also across from Tunnels Beach are the **Waikapalae and Waikanaloa Wet Caves**, which are only partially submerged. Scuba divers can explore them both, but conditions are not very good. The nickname "Tunnels Beach" has caused quite a rift between local extreme adventurers. Scuba divers argue the name comes from the fantastic underwater lava tubes. Surfers hotly dispute this, saying it is named for the tunnel-like waves that break here. Ahhhhhh, troubles in paradise!

Outfitters & Resources

Aquatic Adventures
4-1380 Kuhio Hwy.
Kapa'a, Kauai, HI 96746
☎ 808-822-1434
Full-service dive shop offering rentals,
excursions and certification courses. Large
scuba equipment retail shop.

Hanalei Sea Tours
PO Box 1447
Hanalei, Kauai, HI 96714
☎ 808-826-7254 or 800-733-7997
Full- and half-day Zodiac trips along the
ultra-beautiful Na Pali coastline. Meal and
snorkeling equipment included. Hanalei
also does a catamaran adventure tour.

Inter-Island Helicopters
PO Box 156
Hanapepe, Kauai, HI 96716
☎ 808-335-5009 or 800-245-9696
The search-and-rescue people also do
customized group flights. Aerial
photography options available.

Jack Harter Helicopters

PO Box 306
Lihue, Kauai, HI 96766
☎ 808-245-3774
The oldest and most reputable helicopter business on Kauai. Their motto: "Imitated by all, equaled by none."

Kauai Sea Sports

2827 Poipu Road, Poipu Plaza
Koloa, Kauai, HI 96756
☎ 808-742-9303
Snorkeling and scuba rental and retail shop. Also offers surfing, snorkel and scuba lessons.

Kauai Water Ski and Surf Co.

4-356 Kuhio Hwy.
Kinipopo Shopping Village
Wailua, Kauai, HI 96746
☎ 808-822-3574
The main waterski company on the Wailua River. They also rent kayaks, surfboards, boogie boards, and snorkeling equipment.

Kayak Kauai

PO Box 508
Hanalei, Kauai, HI 96714
☎ 808-826-9844
Ocean kayak tours up the Na Pali Coast, as well as kayak instruction and rental. Day trips and adventure tours; surf and camping gear also available for rent.

Mana Divers
3707 Kikee Road
Kalaheo, Kauai, HI 96741
☎ 808-332-7217
*Full-service dive shop also leads dive
excursions around the whole island.*

Na Pali Eco-Adventures
PO Box 1017
Hanalei, Kauai, HI 96714
☎ 808-826-6804 or 800-659-6804
*Smooth-ride catamaran tours of the Na Pali
Coast. Longer snorkeling time – less travel
time.*

Na Pali Zodiac
PO Box 456
Hanalei, Kauai, HI 96714
☎ 808-826-9371 or 800-422-7824
*Full- and half-day trips along the
ultra-beautiful Na Pali coastline. Beverages
and snorkeling equipment included.*

Ohana Helicopter
3220 Kuhio Hwy., Suite #A
Lihue, Kauai, HI 96766
☎ 808-245-3996 or 800-222-6989
*Personalized helicopter tours by a veteran
pilot who was born on Kauai.*

Outfitters Kauai
2827-A Poipu Road, Poipu Plaza
Poipu Beach, Kauai, HI 96756
☎ 808-742-9667
Offers kayak lessons, tours and rentals.
They also rent mountain bikes.

Po'oku Stables
Po'oku Road
Princeville, Kauai, HI 96722
☎ 808-826-6777
The Po'oku Stables lead horseback journeys
to the top of Kalihiwai Falls and Hanalei
Valley.

Ray's Rentals and Activities
1345 Kuhio Hwy.
Downtown Kapa'a, Kauai, HI 96746
☎ 808-822-5700
Windsurfing, kayak rental gear and other
beach rentals and sales.

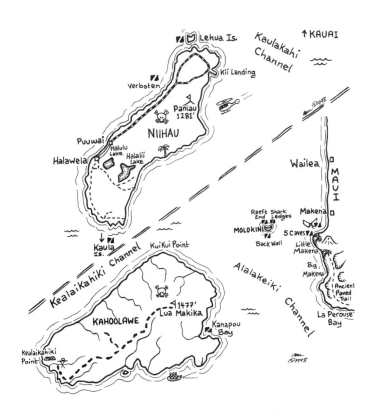

↑ KAUAI

Lehua Is.

Kaulakahi Channel

Kii Landing

Verboten

Paniau 1281'

NIIHAU

Puuwai

Halawela

Halulu Lake

Halalii Lake

Wailea

M A U I

Reefs Shark End Ledges

Makena

MOLOKINI

5 Caves

Back Wall

Little Makena

Kaula Is.

Kealaikahiki Channel

KuiKui Point

Alalakeiki Channel

Big Makena

Ancient Paved Trail

KAHOOLAWE

1477' Lua Makika

Kanapou Bay

La Perouse Bay

Kealaikahiki Point

©1998

FORBIDDEN ISLANDS

"In violence the islands lived, and in violence a great beauty was born." ~ James Michener, Hawaii

The Hawaiian island chain is the most remote land mass in the world. Smack dab in the middle of the North Pacific, the eight main islands are some 2,500 miles from the nearest continent. All the flora and fauna that colonized the islands before the arrival of humans came by air, on ocean currents, or attached to migratory birds. The odds were heavily against any life form making this journey successfully, but time is always on the side of evolution. Those species that managed to survive the transition rapidly diversified and flourished in an equable climate with few competitors. But it's the same old sad story: When the humans and their introduced animals showed up, many indigenous species could not compete and became extinct, or are on the verge of extinction today. There are more endangered species in Hawaii than in all the other Unites States combined.

Species extinction is not the reason two of the eight main Hawaiian islands are forbidden, but it should be. No, this is yet another man-made anomaly. One island is shut off from the rest of the world because a rich white family/corporation wants it that way. The other had been a bombing target island for the U.S. Navy and is so riddled with unexploded ordnance that it is highly dangerous even to set foot on it. Go figure.

Located 17 miles off the coast of Kauai is the small (70-square-mile) island of **Niihau**. It is entirely owned by the descendants of a missionary family, the Robinsons, who prohibit all but invited visitors. While this dictum has been criticized, it is actually the only thing keeping the last vestige of the Hawaiian tradition, culture, race and language pure. Ninety-five percent of Niihauans are pure-blood Hawaiian, and the Hawaiian language is frequently spoken in the home. While only 230 people live on Niihau, what they represent is far more impressive than their numbers. Contrary to popular belief, Niihauans can come and go from the island as they please, yet few choose to relocate elsewhere.

Niihau

SCUBA DIVING THE NIIHAU COAST

Getting to Niihau is one thing. Staying off the island is quite another. Perhaps it's the temptation of venturing onto the "Forbidden Island" just to say you did it. The odd scuba diving party have, on rare occasions, ventured upon the beaches of Niihau for a picnic, only to be run off by angry locals shooting guns into the air. The people of Niihau wish to remain unbothered and alone.

Until recently, it was forbidden for anyone but Niihauans even to get *close* to the island. This meant that dive boats that didn't even want to go ashore were waived off by angry locals. Well, things have lightened up now, and dive companies are presently allowed to make the 17-mile journey across the Kaulakahi Channel from Kauai, as long as they don't land on Niihau. Problem is, the crossing takes three hours one-way and can be attempted only on calm days in the summer. But once here, it's near-virgin diving territory.

Sea critters.

LEHUA ISLAND DIVE

RISK: 4   **ADRENALINE: 5**

Off the northern tip of Niihau is the half-square-mile islet known as Lehua. The islet is completely uninhabited and is regarded as one of the most exceptional dive sites in all of Hawaii. The reason it is so highly esteemed is not the *amount* of coral, but the degree to which it is preserved. Very few dives have been made here, so, as with Niihau itself, everything is preserved the way it's always been.

OTHER NiiHAU DIVE SITES

The coastal areas off the northwest shore of the island offer some prime dive locations. Sites include amazing underwater canyons, steep drop-offs, giant sea arches and spectacular cathedrals, all in near-virgin condition. Because Niihau has been isolated for so long, the marine life in its surrounding waters is abundant and varied. Encounters with white-tip reef sharks, rays, jacks, ulua, tuna and other gamefish are frequent.

Another prime scuba diving location is the islet of **Kaula**, a few miles off the southern tip of Niihau. Known for its plentiful sea life, Kaula is a great dive location, if only you can find an outfitter that will take you all the way out there. (Generally, outfitters are hard to find and will do this trip only by special arrangement; plan ahead.) Lucky for the people of Niihau, the fishing grounds off the island's coast are some of the richest in the whole state of Hawaii.

HELICOPTER FLIGHTS OVER NiiHAU

The fascination of seeing The Forbidden Island up close must be a real temptation for some. Everybody knows that when you tell a person they can't do something, its appeal only becomes greater. Now, those who have a few hundred dollars to burn can take a helicopter flight all around Niihau (except over the two villages where the population is concentrated).

The company that does the flights (**Niihau Helicopter**, Kaumakani, ☎ 808-335-3500) actually has permission to land on a remote beach. Passengers can take a short hike along the shore and thus gain the bragging rights of having walked upon *kapu* (taboo) territory.

Kahoolawe

From the day after the Japanese bombing of Pearl Harbor in 1941, until 1990 when then-president George Bush ordered a halt to all bombing on Kahoolawe, the U.S. Navy had totally thrashed the island by using it as a bombing target. Few life forms exist on the topsoil-depleted island today, apart from a couple of feral goats that continue to eat the remaining vegetation. The U.S. Navy readily admits Kahoolawe is the most bombed piece of land in the entire world (it was, by all accounts, very instrumental in winning the Pacific War). There are so many unexploded shells, above and below the surface, that it is extremely dangerous to walk on the island. The clean-up bill is reported to be in the billions of dollars and will take at least a decade before public access is granted. Although Kahoolawe has now been annexed to Hawaii, it is unclear if the bombed-out archeological sites on this once sacred island will ever be recovered, or if it will become safe for resettlement.

ADVENTURE RAFTING
AROUND KAHOOLAWE

RISK: 8   ADRENALINE: 6

Kahoolawe is 11 miles long and six miles wide, with 29 miles of coastline. It is only eight miles off Maui, yet the closest harbor is several miles farther at Kihei and Waalaea Bay. Adventure rafting outfitters that circumnavigate Kahoolawe exist, but excursions are infrequent and outfitters change often. Try **Blue Water Rafting** at ☎ 808-879-RAFT; or **Ocean Activities Center** at ☎ 808-879-4485.

Those who know how to operate an outboard motor and understand weather patterns and ocean currents well can charter their own craft. Best of all are the durable Zodiac rafts – ideal for getting into tight coves and quick maneuvering. However, it is unlikely anyone will rent you a boat if you tell them you want to go to Kahoolawe. If you do manage to convince them that you know the sea, or have your own craft, this is one hell of an extreme adventure!

Circumnavigating the island is especially rewarding simply because so few people do it. Thus, most of the reefs are virgin territory for diving (just stay clear of anything that might look like a bomb). In addition, the waters are notably abundant with sea life for fishing, and occasional archeological sites can be spotted from the boat. Especially interesting is Kealaikahiki Point, on the island's southwest corner – the name translated means "way to foreign lands." The point served as a navigational aid for sailors venturing to and from Tahiti.

Molokini

DIVING MOLOKINI CRATER

Just offshore Makena on southwestern Maui is little **Molokini Crater**, a crescent-shaped islet formed by an undersea eruption. Cinder cones follow a general line on Maui, extending from Hana to La Perouse Bay, where the rift zone extends farther out into the ocean. In the case of Molokini, hot lava exploded violently from contact with the sea and built up the typical "tuff cone," which has been worn down over the years by wave action. If the ocean levels were to drop, say during another Ice Age, Molokini would once again be connected to Maui.

Molokini Crater is known as one of the top dive spots in the world. The visibility is a constant 100 feet or more, the water is relatively warm year-round, and the sheer number of tropical fish creates a rainbow effect. Look up and marvel at the colorful schools of lemon butterfly fish, chubs, trumpet fishes, surgeons and wrasse. Snorkelers enjoy the fact that some of the coral reef comes to within 10 feet of the surface.

The crater is now a state marine reserve, so all aquatic life is protected and people are not allowed to climb on the exposed portion of the crater, nor take anything out of the water. The result of this protection is some of the most people-friendly fish in the sea, who not only hope you hand-feed them, but entirely expect it. Don't be surprised if you have a few buddies following you around on your dive.

SHARK LEDGES

 RISK: 4 *ADRENALINE: 4*

On the northeastern side of the crescent, the side closest to Maui, is the less popular site known as Shark Ledges. Here, a series of ledges descends like a stairway. The ledges are home to guess what? Yup, sharks. No danger of being munched by these docile white-tip reef sharks, although some can seem frightening because they get rather big. Also big and scary, but not dangerous, are a large number of resident moray eels. This dive is popular as either a deep dive or the beginning of a drift dive along the back wall.

Diving the Back Wall.

MOLOKINI BACK WALL

 RISK: 7   ADRENALINE: 6

Serious divers plan on diving Molokini early in the morning for the best visibility in calm waters before the wind and currents pick up. While the outer rim of the crater is fascinating for skin-divers and intermediate divers alike, most advanced divers make their way to the back side of the crater. Here you will find a vertical wall going 350 feet straight down. Excellent sea life can be spotted on the back side, including small gray sharks, spy rays, yellowfin tuna, trevally jacks, spinner dolphins and other large fish.

WARNING...
Underwater vertigo and "narcing out" are a very real danger on the backside, and divers must monitor their gauges frequently to avoid dropping too deep. Another danger is the strong current, known as the "Tahiti Express," because that's the next stop if you get swept out to sea.

Nihoa & Necker

Two tiny islands past the archipelago of the "Big Eight" are hardly ever mentioned in travel books, much less described with information on how to get there. The two outcroppings beyond Kauai and Niihau are called Nihoa and Necker Islands, and, like the others, they are remnants of volcanoes.

Archeological evidence shows signs of previous inhabitation, particularly on Nihoa, which once supported a population of up to 100 people. But the real mind-blowing aspect of these islands is how *small* they are. While little Niihau boasts 70 square *miles*, Nihoa offers only 156 *acres* and Necker only 39 acres. (An acre equals only 1/640th of a square mile!)

It is hard to imagine a colony of people spending their whole lives on these remote nubbins of rock. But the evidence of that is ample, with 60 archeological sites on Nihoa and 34 on Necker. Several well-built temples remain, as well as a cave that show signs of human occupation. Most striking are the number of unique stone images found nowhere else in Hawaii, but reminiscent of idols from the Marquesas. While mystery remains as to what happened to the peoples of Nihoa and Necker, a lack of food sources and fresh water suggest a tragic human drama. Without timber for new canoes and very limited resources, a protracted drought may have led to widespread starvation. Perhaps this is why the islands are now so barren.

 ## *NIHOA ISLAND EXCURSION*

RISK: 8 ADRENALINE: 5

Nihoa, about 170 miles from Kauai, was first sighted by Europeans in 1789. Like those intrepid navigators of the high seas, you too will have to take to the ocean. There is no known outfitter that charters trips to Nihoa, let alone Necker, which is another 130 miles from Nihoa. Maybe a trip to these islands can be tied into a deep-sea fishing outing, or you can just charter your own craft and swim from the boat. Fishing is limited to the open ocean near the island. This is an excellent spot to drop a line for some deep-sea creatures or to dive a virgin reef.

Nihoa has sea cliffs on all four sides, with no beaches for landings. Nihoa is kinda U-shaped, surrounding a small, deep bay called Adam Bay. All landings must be made on a rocky shelf in Adam Bay, and then only in ideal weather conditions.

A LITTLE RESPECT...

When exploring the island, please be respectful to any artifacts or rock piles you come across. This is living Hawaiian history and should not be disturbed.

Outfitters & Resources

Blue Water Rafting
PO Box 10172
Lahaina, Maui, HI 96761
☎ 808-879-7238
Adventure Zodiac raft trips out to Molokini and Kahoolawe. Meals and snorkeling equipment included.

Bubbles Below
Kapa'a, Kauai, HI 96746
☎ 808-822-3483
Charters scuba and snorkel trips out to Lehua Island off Niihau.

Dive Maui
900 Front Street
Lahina, Maui, HI 96761
☎ 808-667-2080
Foremost tour operator to Molokini Crater and other Maui destinations. Ask about their Molokini backside trips.

Niihau Helicopters
PO Box 370
Makaweli, Kauai, HI 96769
☎ 808-335-3500
Two nonscheduled tourist charters fly over the "Forbidden Island" with a landing on a secluded beach.

SeaEscape U-Drive Boat Rental
1979 S. Kihei Road
Kihei, Maui, HI 96753
☎ 808-879-3721
Rent your own Zodiac or larger boat for 'forbidden' trips out to Molokini or Kahoolawe.

Organizations
& Resources

Aloha Airlines	☎ 800-323-3345
Hawaiian Airlines	☎ 800-882-8811
Hawaii Council of Dive Clubs PO Box 298 Honolulu, Oahu HI, 96809	
Hawaiian Trail & Mountain Club	☎ 808-734-5515
Hawaii Visitors Bureau 2270 Kalakaua Ave., Suite 801 Honolulu, Oahu HI, 96815	☎ 808-923-1811
U.S. Hang Gliding Association	☎ 800-616-6888

ENVIRONMENTAL GROUPS

Division of Forestry and Wildlife
54 S. High Street, Room #101
PO Box 1015
Wailuku, Maui, HI 96793
☎ 808-243-5352, 244-4352

Maui Visions Vacations
3681 Baldwin Avenue
Makawao, HI 96768
visions@maui.net
☎ 808-572-2161 or 800-MAUI-695
Tour herbal habitats, meet elder healers, explore sacred sites, and learn treasured arts.

The Nature Conservancy of Hawaii
1116 Smith Street, Room #201
Honolulu, HI 96817
☎ 808-537-4508
or PO Box 1716
Makawao, Maui HI 96768
☎ 808-572-7849
Inter-island nonprofit conservation organization conducts natural history day hikes. Hawaii's answer to the Sierra Club. Advance reservations required.

Sierra Club
730 Polk Street
San Francisco, CA 94109
☎ 415-923-5630
California environmental group also leads trips to Hawaii.